JOYFUL HEARTS

JOYFUL HEARTS

THE TRANSFORMATIVE POWER OF PRAISE

CAMILLE BURCH

Praise

PUBLISHING

a division of Crazy Praise Club

Cover and Layout Design by Lydia Christine Hall

Illustrations by Ashley Rogers, www.createdministry.com

31 30 29 28 27 26 25   1 2 3 4 5 6 7

ISBN 979-8-9988389-0-3

This book is dedicated to every person who has ever done
a Crazy Praise Club event, study, or workshop over the years.

Every one of you inspires me!

DEDICATED TO MY CPC TRIBE, MENTORS, AND FRIENDS

As it turns out, writing a book does, indeed, take a village. I want to dedicate this book to the key people who helped get this book across the finish line. Without them, it never would have happened.

My community is full of amazing friends and accountability partners. They pushed me to tell this story so that others could benefit from it and they stood by me, even when the going got tough. Thank you to Helen Breier, Donna Whitten Dibble, Chris Dilworth, Kyle Horton, Marcie Lane, Amy South, Carole Townsend, Carla Cooper, Joy Coffey, Jodi Denm and Tristan Luciotti. The Lord used each of you to make sure we pushed forward, so thank you!

I also dedicate this to my Pastor and his wife, Rico and Vikki Ruiz. They are my ministry partners, prayer warriors and financial contributors.

TO MY WATCH AND WRITE CHRISTIAN WRITERS GROUP

These talented writers and podcasters have shared insights, information and resources that made this book possible. They are: Donna Whitten Dibble, Carmen Drew, Amanda Hayhurst, Eve Harrell, Tierra Lebbie, Lauren Sanchez, Laura Shaw and Tracey Axnick.

TO MY MOM

Thanks for making sure I had a strong spiritual foundation early in my life, and for helping bring it back to me later in life. Because of you I have eternal life with Jesus, and I'm forever grateful.

CONTENTS

FOREWARD

I placed my strainer full of strawberries in the sink, lightly spraying them off with the cool water from the faucet. *Maybe making jam will make me feel better.* Plopping my cutting board on the counter, I took the strawberries one by one and sliced off the tops, cutting them down the middle and tossing them into a bowl. Although my body may have been physically standing in my kitchen, my mind was anything but present.

Just weeks prior, I received earthshattering news that our precious little boy Reese had leukemia. At that point, we still didn't know what his fate would be. A rare genetic chromosome complicated his prognosis, making his treatment even more aggressive. We were in survival mode, and I was struggling to just get from one day to the next.

It was in those weeks and months after Reese's diagnosis that I found a lifeline—one that got me through some of my darkest days: *praise*. Crying out to God lifted me from the pain of my circumstances to the supernatural comfort of His promises, just as it did on that late afternoon in my kitchen.

Lifting my hands toward the sky, I belted out the lyrics of "Here Again" by Elevation Worship from the deepest part of my soul:

> *Can't go back to the beginning.*
> *Can't control what tomorrow will bring.*
> *But I know here in the middle*
> *Is a place where You promise to be.*

With tears streaming down my face, I kept singing:

> *I'm not enough unless You come.*
> *Will You meet me here again?*

Foreward

'Cause all I want is all You are.
Will You meet me here again?

It was praise that got me through this most painful season—and not just songs of praise but, much like you will read in this book, anything I could do to draw near to God and pour out what I had at His feet.

I literally had stacks of journals and tabs of notes on my phone to capture all I was pouring out: My lament. My thanksgiving. My questions—*oh so many questions.* The countless stories of God's people meeting our daily needs. The glimpses of beauty. My fears and worries. My deep, overflowing joy when the cancer was no longer found.

And I can't forget the hike up Mount Yona in Northeast Georgia with my brother and sister-in-law. With every turn and ascension, I was a step closer to the prize awaiting me—a view so spectacular I had to sit down to fully soak in its beauty. Being outside made me feel closer to God. The vibrant colors, the tall mountain peaks, the vast wildlife.

See, that's what praise does—it sets our eyes on the One who is worthy of it. It lifts us from our circumstances. It draws us closer to Him.

I am so grateful for this book and for my incredible friend who wrote it. Camille will expand your view of praise in the most exciting ways. What once felt mundane and ordinary will feel exciting again, or perhaps exciting for the very first time. Get ready because the Crazy Praise Club is about to welcome its newest member—*you.*

Amanda Hayhurst
Author of bestselling devotionals *Pray for Him* and *Pray for Her*

INTRODUCTION:
WELCOME TO THE CRAZY PRAISE CLUB

I magine a club that expands across denominations and cultures, gathering like-minded individuals who share a passion for praising God in unique and personalized ways. Scripture reveals an important truth: God delights in our praise and desires a deep, intimate relationship with each of us. This very relationship fuels our creativity, as we understand that our worship should be as unique as the bond we share with Him.

Throughout the Bible, we find countless examples of God's people expressing their worship creatively. From David's exuberant dancing before the Lord to the psalmists' use of musical instruments, the artisans crafting beautiful artwork for the temple, and the woman pouring perfume on Jesus's feet, we see that our worship can take many forms. Why can't we push the boundaries of worship ourselves? The answer is we can and God wants that! (We may even pour out expensive perfume!)

Over a decade ago, a number of kindred spirits found each other in a Bible study. We were bound by our desire to deepen our faith and encounter God in an unprecedented way. I was honored to be a part of that group. Our first adventure was a jubilant picnic and devotional, followed by a trek to the base of Tallulah Gorge. With pen and paper, we scribbled all the obstacles hindering our spiritual growth and set them ablaze as we ascended from the depths of the gorge. With hearts free of those burdens, we rejoiced that we had symbolically released ourselves from past struggles. On that triumphant journey out of the gorge, we coined the name Crazy Praise Club. That name is a fitting representation of our boldness and devotion to moving forward in community toward expressions of praise that would stretch and grow us in our faith.

Crazy Praise Club is not just a catchy name but a movement—a community of believers who yearn to put our faith in motion as praise. Together, we explore innovative ways to express our love and worship of God, stepping beyond the familiar and embracing our own unique languages of praise. When we do, we transform our faith and learn more about Christ's character. He is an incredibly innovative, loving, fun, and available Savior. We can discover fresh pathways to intimacy with Him when we explore the limitless possibilities for expressing our praise.

The Lord even cared enough about the reader experience to connect me with an amazing artist, Ashley Rogers, prophetic artist and founder of www. createdministry.com. Her sensitivity to the Holy Spirit's leading with the illustrations has added depth and richness to the book. Our Joyful Hearts devotional features more of Ashley's writing and art.

Crazy Praise Club: A Journey of Trust

When we first embarked on this adventure known as Crazy Praise Club, we didn't know where it would lead us. We desired to deepen our faith and experience God in new and exciting ways, but the specific path was unclear. As we journeyed together, we quickly realized that this journey would require trust—trust in ourselves, trust in one another, and most importantly, trust in God.

Trusting ourselves meant stepping out of our comfort zones and being open to trying new things. For some of us, this meant picking up a paintbrush for the first time or singing in front of others. It meant being vulnerable and sharing our passions and talents. As we trusted ourselves more, we discovered hidden depths within ourselves that we never knew existed.

Each of us had to push beyond our existing boundaries in different ways. God wanted us to grow in community, not isolate ourselves. We had each just emerged from emotionally unhealthy situations, and we hoped for a future radically different from where we found ourselves. We were all in need of profound healing and sought to open new pathways to experience Jesus and His joy that restores. We placed our trust in God as that Healer and Giver of joy.

I mentioned trusting ourselves and God, but trusting one another was also crucial on this journey. We were venturing into uncharted territory together, and it required us to be vulnerable with each other. We had to put aside insecurities and judgments. We learned to embrace and support each other's unique expressions of worship. Through this process, strong bonds formed between us—bonds rooted in love, acceptance, and a mutual understanding that our differences only added richness to our experiences.

Along the journey, our healing required us to be honest about some of our past sins, poor choices, and insecurities. We shared things that to this day remain in confidence between group members. As we were honest and able to let go of past hurts and patterns, freedom and truth in life facilitated freedom in praise.

The bonds we built have stood the test of circumstances—breakups, cross-country moves, joyful reconciliations, and tragic ends. We've had seasons when we were incredibly close and also stretches of time when there was, necessarily, more distance. When one of our members lost his father to Covid, we gathered at the celebration of life. At that time, we had not all been together for several years. Yet, after the funeral, we were the final ones there, praying and weeping together as we had done so many times before.

Initially, we thought Crazy Praise Club might be for a season or even a few years. But we've learned that our Crazy Praise Club bond is, in fact, for a lifetime. And now, you are invited to be part of this movement. My prayer for you is that you, too, experience life-altering growth as a result of embracing new practices in praise.

Building Each Other Up: The Gift of Exhortation

Going back to those early years of our journey with Crazy Praise Club, one gift that stood out powerfully was exhortation. Romans 12:8 mentions this gift, also known as encouragement or edification, as one of God's spiritual gifts to His people. It was evident that each club member possessed this gift in abundance.

Our club was a breath of fresh air in a world where negativity and criticism seem to be the norm. We prioritized constantly building each other up and speaking life-giving words into one another's lives. Whenever someone shared their struggles or insecurities, someone else was always ready with an encouraging word or a reminder of their unique gifts and strengths.

We realized that many of us had come from backgrounds where we were constantly torn down and made to feel worthless. That is true of many people in life. But through the gift of exhortation, we created a safe space where everyone felt valued and appreciated for who they were. This strengthened our bond as a group and helped each grow in confidence and self-worth.

We always spoke truth to one another even when it was hard, but truth always came from a place of love and empathy, never from judgment. We worked hard to set up healthy boundaries and to be safe people so that we could enjoy healthy relationships, as we had learned in the Bible study where we met, which was called Divorce Care. We practiced with one another by building safe friendships as a place to start.

So, mutual respect and exhortation became one of the pillars of the Crazy Praise Club experience. My hope is that you will find a place where you can feel safe, be exhorted, experience encouragement, and hear God's life-giving words, whether it is through reading this book or in the context of your own Crazy Praise Club group.

The Power of Acknowledgment

One aspect of exhortation that stood out to the original Crazy Praise Club group was the power of acknowledgment. We made it a habit not just to give general words of encouragement but to acknowledge each person's strengths and abilities specifically. This could be anything from complimenting some-one's singing voice or artistic skills to acknowledging their wisdom or leader-ship qualities or actively appreciating their gift of hospitality.

We found that this simple act profoundly impacted people's lives. One member shared with us how she had always felt inadequate and useless. However, after being acknowledged for her talent in writing, she began to see herself in a new light and even started pursuing her writing passion more confidently.

In another instance, when one member opened up about her struggles with anxiety, the rest of us were quick to remind her of the strength and resil-ience she exhibited in overcoming her fears. Personally, I struggled with my identity as an individual after entering into one unhealthy relationship after another. I discovered an identity in Christ, not in another person, and for the first time, I felt free. Crazy Praise Club became the catalyst for so much positive change in so many areas of life.

Perhaps the most crucial aspect of trust on this journey was learning to trust God fully. As individuals from different backgrounds and experiences, our understandings of who God is varied significantly. Yet, as we opened ourselves up to His guidance and direction through prayer and study of His Word, we each discovered deeper intimacy with Him, each in our own way.

One particular season exemplifies how trusting God led us on an incredible journey. Our group embarked on a mission trip to an inner-city homeless shelter to prepare and serve Christmas dinner. None of us had ever undertaken anything like this before, but God compelled us to take this step of faith. As we spent Christmas day talking with the workers and residents of the shelter, God used the time to show us that joy can be so simple—it can be found in a good meal, for example, or a meaningful conversation, or prayer time.

Those incredibly exhilarating experiences lingered for years, fueling countless interactive praise sessions. They linger still. Each person and memory is a precious gem polished by fond remembrance and love. The ways God has shown me to draw close to Him have come from unexpected places, and that is exactly what I hope you discover as you encounter the Crazy Praise Club approach to praise. During the duration of the original Crazy Praise Club, I got a sense from God that when the time was right, we would move far beyond our group to touch other lives. I knew that was not yet the time. However, when I was seeking God in prayer and fasting in the beginning of 2024, I felt the nudge that the time is now. He gave me this book, which I was not expecting, and the go-ahead to work on a ministry with live events and online content. And so, I began. When I lost my job a few months after, I really dove in and was able to complete the book in a matter of months.

Now, the Crazy Praise Club team (which is several spiritual advisors and myself) is working on an online course and workbook, along with a small-group study guide, all built around the idea of broadening our concept of praise. The memories and inspiring stories of our joyful gatherings provide the fuel for this book, and I can't wait to share our ideas with you. So, now you're caught up with the Crazy Praise Club story!

Which brings us back to you. You are invited to embrace your God-given creativity, explore the endless possibilities of praising Him, and have fun building community as you put your faith in motion, using the insights we were so blessed to gain in our initial group. Now that you know the Crazy Praise Club story, it's time to join us and craft *your* story, one that's unique to you and your journey with Jesus. So, let's get started. Welcome to Crazy Praise Club!

UNDERSTANDING INTIMACY WITH GOD

Here's some excellent news to start with—God is beckoning you into a deeper relationship with Him! You are here seeking that as well, inviting God to be at the center of your life's journey. When you earnestly seek Him, He promises to make Himself known. As you seek intimacy with God and He reveals Himself to you, you may find yourself wanting to express your praise in ways that are uniquely yours but go beyond what you have experienced before. At the same time, you will discover that expressing praise in your unique way deepens the intimacy. This is a beautiful cycle of praise and intimacy.

As you embark on this journey of understanding intimacy with God, pause and consider what true intimacy means. Intimacy is more than just knowing facts about God or following religious rituals. It's about developing a deep, personal relationship with the Creator of the universe.

Imagine sitting with your closest friend and sharing your deepest thoughts and feelings. You find comfort, vulnerability, and a sense of being known and accepted. Now, magnify that a thousandfold, and you will begin to understand the intimacy God desires with you.

But how do we cultivate this intimacy? It starts with an open heart and a willingness to listen. Prayer becomes focused on an honest, two-way conversation. Meditation involves focusing our minds and tuning our hearts to God's frequency. Then, we can embrace gratitude, joyful celebration, and the happiness that comes from a community of love. Let's make this journey active, exuberantly seeking God and joyously honoring Him in all we do!

But here's a warning. This takes some effort on our part. It requires us not only to talk but to listen. Many years ago, my life was in shambles. I went through a divorce, and the pain of that experience caused me to run far away from God. I jumped into a rebound relationship that filled me with shame and also failed after many years. I was at the end of myself, and I knew my

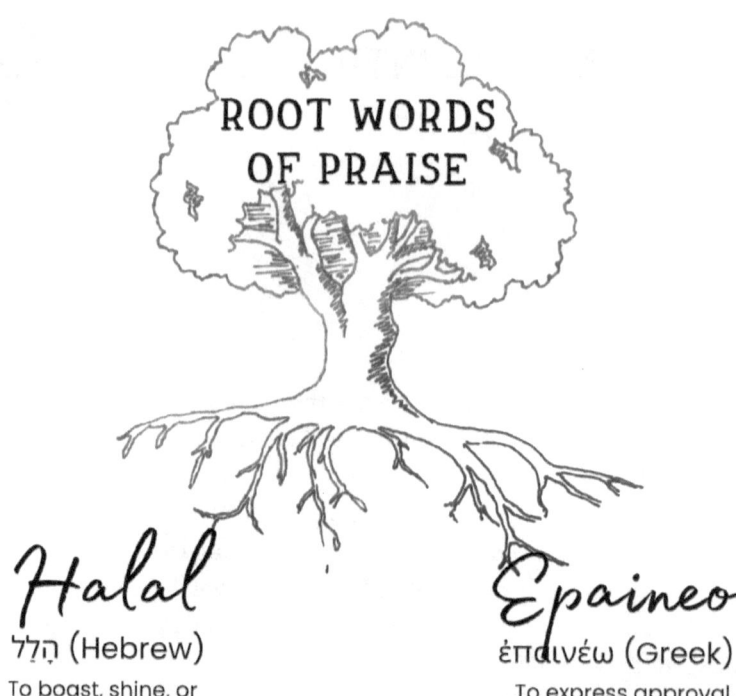

ROOT WORDS OF PRAISE

Halal
הָלַל (Hebrew)

To boast, shine, or celebrate God publicly

-Used over 160 times in the Old Testament

-The word "Hallelujah" is a compound word of halal (praise) + "Yah" (Yaweh) found in Psalms

Psalms 113:1- "Praise (halal) the Lord, Praise! O servants of the Lord, praise the name of the Lord."

Epaineo
ἐπαινέω (Greek)

To express approval, commend, or celebrate virtue

-Frequently used in the New Testament

-Epaineo combines "epi" (upon) and "animo" (to praise)

Romans 15:11- "Praise (espaineo) the Lord all you Gentiles and let all the people extol Him."

Ephesians 1:8 "To the praise (espaineo) of the glory of His grace."

only way back to peace, happiness, and freedom was to return to the God who had never left me. It was I who had chosen to go, not Him.

James 4:8 says, "Come near to God and He will come near to you. Wash your hands, you sinners, and purify your hearts, you double-minded." This Scripture clearly states there must be intent on our part. I was at a crossroads. It was time for me to take action to regain that intimacy with God that my spirit craved.

Completely broken and unsure of what to do next, I cried out to God on my family-room floor, heaving tears of regret and shame. Though I wasn't hearing clearly from God then, I remember feeling that if I trusted Him, He would take me back. He would help me rebuild my life into a life of significance. He showed me a vision of a rickety old brick wall, which represented my life. Together, we dismantled the old wall brick by brick. But then, *He* rebuilt it with shiny new bricks, and it was perfect and solid.

And I chose to trust Him because His love is unfailing, and we rejoiced together in my return to His family. Though I had hard work ahead of me (the dismantling was rough, trust me!), a peace washed over me as I began my long journey back. I decided to draw near to God so He would come near to me. I clung to that promise through pain and tears, the ripping away of things that didn't belong, grieving the necessary abandonment of unhealthy relationships, the loss of loved ones during this season, and a feeling of isolation that I had to overcome somehow.

In this context, I first attended the small group that birthed Crazy Praise Club. Everyone in that group was broken, seeking a fresh touch from God and needing deep emotional healing. The Lord is so kind. He was there for us and provided healing through praise in ways unique to each of our journeys. All the activities we did in those early days of Crazy Praise Club right through to the present day are God's creative ideas. As the group grew and I taught CPC to other groups or individuals, those others offered ideas for things they did that were meaningful. Some ideas sprang from individual giftings or talents, and many were ideas that came from Scripture. But no matter the source, the healing they set in motion was profound and real.

You Are Uniquely Created to Worship Your Creator

As we continue this journey toward more profound intimacy with God through praise, we must understand that each of us is uniquely created. We have different personalities, styles, and preferences when connecting with God. This beautiful revelation means our worship and praise can also be unique and personal.

But that's not to say you are to be stuck in a rut where you are comfortable. In fact, I encourage you to push beyond your default boundaries and adventure into uncharted spiritual territory—you never know what you might find! If you are a nature lover, for example, there are a million different ways and places to worship in nature. If you love art, there is no limit to how artistic you can be for Jesus. For myself, as a writer, I find when I experience God in new ways it fuels my writing and teaching, so I'm always looking for fresh God encounters in all kinds of places.

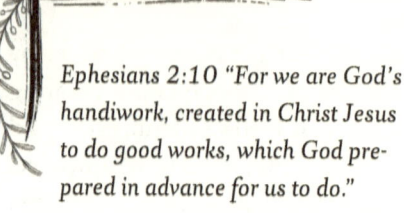

Ephesians 2:10 "For we are God's handiwork, created in Christ Jesus to do good works, which God prepared in advance for us to do."

Ephesians 2:10 reminds us that we are God's handiwork, created in Christ Jesus to do good works, which God prepared us to do. This means He made us unique and has specific purposes and callings unique to each of us.

So, how does our unique gifting relate to our practice of praise? The way we connect with God will also be unique. Some may find solace in quiet contemplation, while others may feel a deep connection through expressive dance or creative arts. Some may connect with God through nature, while others find their most profound moments of worship within the walls of a church building. Some love music, art, or writing, while others find purpose as problem solvers or organizing projects. These are areas of our lives suited to our natures where we are invited to experience God in new ways.

As we learned, the root words for "praise" mean to celebrate, commend, or express approval. When we spend time enjoying nature, for example, we are expressing approval—or praising. When we celebrate a life event with friends, we are praising. In James, we are told that every good gift comes from the Father. So, in fact, anytime we enjoy any good activity, we are praising the Lord and making a connection with Him whether we recognize it or not.

Understanding your unique wiring and how you best connect with God can significantly enhance your praise practice. It allows you to fully embrace yourself and use your gifts and strengths to honor and glorify God. A good way

My Unique Giftings

Did you know you are uniquely equipped to worship God? In the chart below, list or draw some of your unique giftings.

MY SPIRITUAL GIFTS

MY GOD-GIVEN TALENTS

OTHER PEOPLE SAY I DO THIS WELL

MY FAVORITE ATTRIBUTES OF GOD, JESUS AND HOLY SPIRIT

MY SACRED PATHWAY

HOW I LIKE TO WORSHIP

Sacred Pathways

THE NATURALIST:
Enjoys connecting with God outdoors through nature.

THE SENSATE:
Engages spiritually through the five senses and physical experiences.

THE TRADITIONALIST:
Values ritual and structured practices, such as Communion and hymns.

THE ASCETIC:
Prefers solitude and simplicity in spiritual expression.

THE ACTIVIST:
Feels closer to God through justice and social action.

THE CAREGIVER:
Connects with God through acts of service and compassion.

THE ENTHUSIAST:
Loving God with mystery (seeking God's will) and celebration (joyful enthusiasm).

THE CONTEMPLATIVE:
Loving God through adoration, feeling Him in the quiet.

THE INTELLECTUAL:
Enjoys learning about God through study and understanding.

If you search online for Sacred Pathways Assessment, you can find on online Q&A test that will help you identify your sacred pathway.

to get started is with the Sacred Pathways chart below. This helpful tool comes from the book *Sacred Pathways*, by Gary Thomas. In it, he explores eight different spiritual pathways that individuals can follow to deepen their relationship with God and grow in their faith. Though the book is nearly thirty years old, the material is so fresh and vibrant that it still carries meaning today.

It is likely that you will relate to multiple categories, and some others will not be in your wheelhouse at all. These pathways are designed to resonate with different personality types and spiritual temperaments, and each naturally leads to methods for connecting with God, such as through worship, service, contemplation, or study. By identifying which pathway aligns with your natural inclinations and spiritual needs, you can engage in practices that foster a deeper sense of connection and purpose in your life. Applying these pathways involves embracing practices that resonate with you personally, whether through prayer, community service, or meditation, allowing you to integrate your spirituality into everyday life in a meaningful and authentic way.

Having recognized that there are different ways of connecting with God that suit our individual temperaments, we can also experience Him when we step out of those areas and try things that don't feel comfortable at first. This is all part of stretching ourselves so we can grow.

Spiritual Gifts and Praise

The Holy Spirit gives spiritual gifts to build up the body of Christ (1 Corinthians 12:7). These gifts are tools or abilities that enable us to serve others in the church and bring glory to God. As with the sacred pathways above, you may find you have been given more than one gift.

In Romans 12:6–8, Paul lists more gifts—prophecy, serving, teaching, encouraging, giving, leadership, and mercy, to name a few. There is a third list of gifts in Ephesians. As you read through these descriptions, think about how they could play into your practice of praise. For example, someone with the gift of teaching may find joy in leading a Bible study on the power of praise (or even a study based on this book!).

When it comes to the gifts of the Holy Spirit, there are three different lists in the Bible, and they describe the spiritual gifts slightly differently. Utilizing your spiritual gifts regularly is a way to honor the Holy Spirit and to enable His power to accomplish His purposes through you. Your gifts may change and develop over time, so take time to reassess yearly and see if anything has changed.

As I present these lists, please keep in mind we are to use our gifts for four reasons:

HOW TO USE YOUR GIFTS

1. *Edification of the church.* Spiritual gifts are intended to build up and strengthen the church community (Ephesians 4:12).
2. *Service to others.* Spiritual gifts empower believers to serve one another and fulfill God's mission on earth (1 Corinthians 12:11).
3. *Manifestation of God's presence.* Gifts serve as a way to sense God's presence and power, reinforcing faith and encouraging unity (1 Corinthians 12:4–7).
4. *Witness to the world.* Gifts are a testimony to nonbelievers, demonstrating the reality of God's kingdom and work among His followers (1 Corinthians 14:24–25).

Motivational Gifts
Spirit-empowered Passion and Talent

Prophecy. The gift of prophecy is the ability to speak truth boldly, often with a focus on righteousness and calling others to align with God's holy standards. Those with this gift are sensitive to moral issues and have a deep sense of right and wrong.

Service. The gift of service is about helping others through practical acts of service. Those with this gift find joy in meeting the material needs of others and often work behind the scenes to support causes.

Teaching. The gift of teaching is the ability to clearly explain and communicate God's Word. Those with this gift enjoy studying Scripture and helping others understand and apply biblical truths.

Exhortation. The gift of exhortation is about encouraging, comforting, and motivating others to grow in their faith and persevere through challenges. Those with this gift inspire others to live out their faith in confidence.

Giving. The gift of giving is the ability and desire to give generously and cheerfully to meet the needs of others and support the work of God. Those with this gift are often resourceful and find joy in furthering God's kingdom through their generosity.

Leadership. The gift of leadership is about organizing others with diligence and care. Those with this gift have a vision for the future and the ability to guide and inspire people to common goals.

Mercy. The gift of mercy is about showing compassion and empathy to those who are hurting. People with this gift are drawn to those in distress and find fulfillment in offering comfort and support.

Ministry Gifts
Leadership Roles for the Church

Apostles. Apostles are pioneers and spiritual leaders who establish and oversee churches, provide direction, and lay the foundation for Christian communities.

Prophets. Prophets are those who speak God's truth and provide guidance, encouragement, and correction through divine revelation and God's Word.

Evangelists. Evangelists are called to spread the gospel, lead people to Christ, and equip others to share their faith—whether in groups or one-on-one.

Pastors. Pastors are shepherds who care for, nurture, and protect the spiritual well-being of the church community. They prioritize meeting the needs of others.

Teachers. Teachers explain and instruct others in the Word of God, helping believers to grow in understanding and maturity.

Manifestation Gifts
Supernatural Displays of the Spirit

Word of wisdom. This is the ability to apply spiritual truths practically and wisely.

World of knowledge. This is insight and understanding of spiritual matters or truths. (Those with this gift must be sure to maintain confidentiality when sharing their word with others.)

Faith. This is extraordinary trust in God's power and promises beyond what is normal.

Gifts of healing. This is the ability to bring about physical, emotional, or spiritual healing through the empowerment of the Holy Spirit.

Working of miracles. This is the ability to perform supernatural acts with God's power.

Prophecy. This is speaking God's message to encourage, edify, or correct others. (Those with this gift must be sure to always correct others with love.)

Discerning of spirits. This is the ability to recognize whether something is from God, our own flesh, or demonic influence.

Tongues. This is speaking in languages unknown to the speaker but inspired by the Holy Spirit.

Interpretation of tongues. This is the ability to interpret the unknown language of the one speaking in tongues.

A No-Judgment Zone

As you explore new avenues of praise in yourself as well as seek to encourage others, it is important to do so without judgment. My best friend's talents and giftings are completely opposite of mine. She is an extreme introvert while I am an extrovert. She likes one-on-one events whereas I enjoy larger groups. She's highly analytical and data driven whereas I'm a creative. She likes behind-the-scenes activities whereas I don't mind being up front. Early on in our friendship, we made the agreement to appreciate and support one another in our differences. In doing so, we are each free to be who God created us to be. I don't spend my time trying to change her, nor does she try to change me. In fact, we have come to admire and compliment one another's gifts and encourage each other in them.

My friend's words are measured, and when she speaks, I listen. Recently, I did a teaching at a group she was a part of. Afterwards, she wrote me a note that simply said, "Great job—you amaze me!" I teared up because her love, support, and daily prayers have been an undergirding of spiritual support for me over many years, and she is a woman guarded in her praise. That note meant the world to me—in fact, it may be hanging on my fridge right now!

This story demonstrates how important it is to guard against comparing your gifts to others. Even among those with similar gifts, those gifts may manifest in your lives in completely different ways, and that's okay. God is working through each of us as He sees fit. I don't want to spend my time wishing I were like someone else when God created me to be *me* and wants to use my gifts in my own unique way.

Embarking on a Unique New Journey

As we embark on this journey, we must recognize that this is not just about learning new techniques or following a set of rules. It is about opening our hearts to a deeply personal and transformative relationship with our Creator.

When we praise God in new ways, we open our minds to new aspects of who God is, perhaps knowing Him in ways we never have before. We are taking every thought captive for Christ. Intimacy with God can be found in moments of quiet contemplation. But it can go further as we learn to carry an awareness of God's presence into every aspect of our lives. We can come to see the world through His eyes, feel His heart for His creation, and align our will with His.

As you consider new ways to praise Him and set your faith in motion, you learn more about who the person of Christ is. Expect your journey to be filled with profound joy, extraordinary revelation, and even healing tears.

You have a fresh opportunity to praise God and build intimacy with Him daily. A great

Psalm 139:1–4 "You have searched me, LORD, and You know me. You know when I sit and when I rise; You perceive my thoughts from afar. You discern my going out and my lying down; You are familiar with all my ways. Before a word is on my tongue, You, LORD, know it completely."

place to start your journey is the "search-me" prayer found in Psalm 139:1–4. "You have searched me, LORD, and You know me. You know when I sit and when I rise; You perceive my thoughts from afar. You discern my going out and my lying down; You are familiar with all my ways. Before a word is on my tongue, You, LORD, know it completely." Begin your journey by asking the Holy Spirit to be an intimate part of it. Can you ask Him to show you how to surrender all areas of your life to Him? Enjoy the process—it will be amazingly fulfilling.

Write It Down!

It is vitally important to document your journey, so I strongly encourage journaling and writing, and there is a reason behind it. There is power in writing something down. My Christian writer's group taught me about this a few years back, and it's so true.

Habakkuk 2:2–3 says, "Write down the revelation and make it plain on tablets so that a herald may run with it. For the revelation awaits an appointed time; it speaks of the end and will not prove false. Though it linger, wait for it; it will certainly come and will not delay."

This passage emphasizes the importance of writing down visions or revelations clearly so that they can be communicated effectively. It highlights patience and faith in the fulfillment of God's promises, encouraging us as believers to trust in the timing of these revelations. You will enjoy revisiting the revelations God gives you through this book as you continue to build on these practices.

Try getting a clean notebook or journal to use as you work through this book, and see if it makes a difference for you. It may be a practice you wish to continue. If that's the case, we have journaling prompts and thought starters on our website at www.crazypraiseclub.com to get you started. A journal with dedicated space for devotions and reflections can also be a great tool. Sometimes getting started is the hardest part, so take that first step.

Begin by documenting the sacred pathways, spiritual gifts, and "search-me" prayer nudgings that Holy Spirit has revealed thus far. It will be a great foundation for what's to come!

IT'S TIME FOR CRAZY PRAISE!

Here are a few ideas to get you started on your worship journey.

1. **INTIMACY REFLECTION JOURNAL.** Write reflections on personal experiences of God's presence and love. Recall times in your life when you felt incredibly close to God. Why do you think that was the case? What actions can you take to draw closer to Him? Add this journal prompt to your daily Bible reading for new revelations.

2. **PERSONAL PRAYER WALK**. Take a solitary walk in nature, focusing on prayer and openness to God's voice. Pause to admire God's handiwork in vegetation, animals, water, and sky. Ask yourself what God speaks to you personally through His creation and how you can best honor that. Find a quiet place on your walk to read Scripture (even if only on your phone) and spend time in prayer. If you feel bold, sing some songs of praise and dance in the woods!

3. **SPIRITUAL GIFTS TEST**. I recommend consulting God in prayer and even talking to others to determine your spiritual gifts. You can further refine your list by googling "spiritual gifts test" and taking an online test. Your gifting will guide you in some of the best ways you may choose to worship. A good starting point will be reviewing the lists on page 8–10 of this chapter. For example, I have the gift of hospitality. I enjoy inviting brothers and sisters to my home to share a meal and discuss what the Lord is doing in our lives. Often, these gatherings include prayer. Working within your giftings as a foundation from which to expand into new territory is always a great starting point.

MY SPIRITUAL GIFTS

4. **HEART MAPPING.** Begin by gathering colorful markers, a blank sheet of paper, and a quiet space for reflection. Reflect on moments when you felt God's presence or experienced His intimacy. Start by drawing a large heart in the center of the paper to symbolize your heart. Then, around the heart, draw branches extending outward, each representing a specific instance of divine intimacy. Use colors to distinguish different emotions or types of experiences. Write brief descriptions or key words on each branch to capture the essence of those moments. Take time with this process, allowing your heart map to unfold organically as you recall and honor these sacred connections with God.

MY HEART MAP

This heart is a creative self-portrait of your inner life - what fills your heart, fuels your joy, and matters most to you. Use colors, doodles, or icons to represent your feelings. You may choose to divide it into sections or zones to include: people, dreams and goals, identity in Christ, spiritual gifts, bible verses or values, and life purpose.

THE SCIENCE OF PRAISE AND WORSHIP

The world of praise and worship and its impact on the human psyche and physical being are fascinating. In this chapter, I will take you on a journey to uncover the mysteries of how worship influences and shapes us, delving into its psychological and physiological effects on individuals. This will be a very broad overview. Many books on this topic go into depth on the workings of the brain, but I want you to understand why your exercise of praise is so incredibly transformative.

Early on, as we contemplated developing experiences for our original Crazy Praise Club, I was inspired by Dr. Caroline Leaf, a Christian cognitive neuroscientist, author, and speaker known for her work on the mind-brain connection. I had the privilege of hearing Dr. Leaf speak at a women's conference. I remember her

> 2 Cor 10:5 "We demolish arguments and every pretension that sets itself up against the knowledge of God, and take captive every thought to make it obedient to Christ."

saying that a single Scripture inspired her entire career: 2 Corinthians 10:5, which instructs us to take every thought captive for Christ. She said, and I quote because it stuck with me all these years later, "Why would God command us to take every thought captive for Christ if it weren't possible to do so?" Her entire career is built on research around how we can ignite different parts of the brain, with the understanding that God has given us the power to control our thoughts! Dr. Leaf is an academic, so her books are pretty weighty and packed with science and research, but it's fascinating to see how she links individual brain activity to divine intervention.

Understanding the Brain
Sensation and Perception Centers

The brain is highly complex and not fully understood. However, science does know that different areas of the brain are activated and light up with activity according to the stimulus it is recieving. In this highly simplified diagram, notice how very different areas of the brain are activated according to the activity or sensation coming in. You are invited to explore this concept more throughly as you understand how to take every thought captive for Christ!

Parietal Lobe
Processes senory input from touch, sight, and sound. Process spacial locations.

Occipital Lobe
Vison Center - Processes light, color, movement, depth and shape

Frontal Lobe
Thinking & Problem solving
Decision making
Emotions
Personality

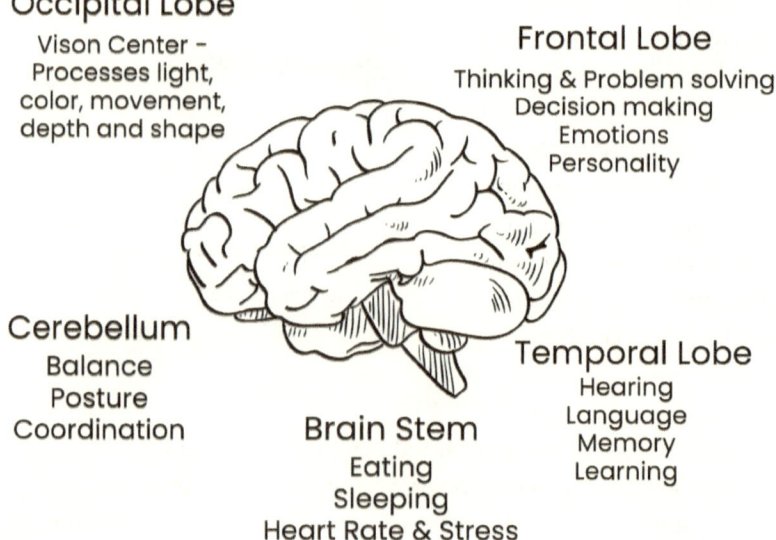

Cerebellum
Balance
Posture
Coordination

Temporal Lobe
Hearing
Language
Memory
Learning

Brain Stem
Eating
Sleeping
Heart Rate & Stress

Diagram compiled with information from the Dana Foundation, a nonprofit dedicated to scientific study and education materials relating to brain function.

Dr. Leaf elaborates on the intricate dance within our brains, revealing that vibrant hues of color and melodious musical notes awaken distinct regions. At the same time, social interactions ignite a symphony of neural connections. She emphasizes that stepping into the unknown sparks a dazzling display of neural fireworks, illustrating how novelty fuels our brain's vitality. By nurturing positive thoughts, mastering new skills, and accomplishing tasks, we illuminate neurotransmitters and sculpt a beautiful landscape of cognitive flourishing.

Within myself, I notice that sometimes, in particular situations, an incredible peace and joy wash over me when I worship in a unique or new place. One occasion when this happened to me was, believe it or not, when I visited a monastery. One of the brothers was teaching us the practices of prayer, and he taught a prayer technique that changed how I usher in God's presence. The technique involved visualizing one's spirit going up a spiritual elevator and finally entering into God's presence. Using his method, I sat in the presence of God like I never had before. I felt I was in the throne room, bowing before the Almighty Himself. It was a powerful experience.

Worship has long been linked to improved well-being. Countless studies have shown how engaging in acts of prayer can reduce stress, anxiety, and depression. Even closing one's eyes and bowing one's head in worship can trigger a physiological response, calming the mind and slowing the breath. This leads to peace and tranquility as heart rate and blood pressure stabilize. Furthermore, the social aspect of worship cannot be overstated. Gathering with like-minded individuals in a place of worship creates a sense of community and belonging. It provides an opportunity for people to connect, share their experiences, and support one another, fostering a sense of unity and camaraderie.

The physiological benefits of worship are equally profound. Singing in unison has been shown to release endorphins, creating a sense of euphoria and heightened emotional connection. Additionally, the physical movements and postures often associated with worship, such as kneeling, bowing, lifting hands, or dancing, can engage and stimulate the body, improving physical health and energy levels.

Worship also significantly deepens an individual's spiritual life. Through it, people can find a deeper connection to their faith, enhancing their spiritual experiences. This may involve a heightened sense of awareness, feeling in tune with the divine, or a profound sense of peace and contentment. Worship allows individuals to explore and express their unique spiritual paths, fostering a sense of purpose and meaning.

17

The brain thrives on new experiences, challenging tasks, and novel ideas. Our brains light up with activity when we engage in these activities as new neural connections are formed. This increases cognitive flexibility, allowing us to think outside the box and approach problems differently.

Dr. Leaf emphasizes that this principle applies to our daily lives and spiritual journeys. While traditions and routines have their place, she encourages individuals to break away from these patterns and experience God in new ways.

One way to do this is through the practice of gratitude. Studies have shown that cultivating gratitude can improve mental health and overall well-being. By intentionally focusing on the positive aspects of our lives, we train our brains to look for good things, even in challenging situations.

Another powerful tool for embracing novelty is cultivating curiosity and exploration. By being curious about the world, we open ourselves to new experiences and ideas, expanding our understanding of God and His creation. Most importantly, we can see the person of Christ at work in the world around us in ways we never expected.

Our ministry, Crazy Praise Club, promotes these principles by offering unique worship experiences to encourage people to break out of their comfort zones and try new ways of connecting with God. Many of these activities are presented in this book. Through creative expressions such as arts, nature, scripture memorization, actively building community, pursuing study topics, practicing active listening, finding new ways to serve others, or whatever suits their unique temperament, individuals can express their faith in ways they may not have thought possible.

These practices stimulate neural growth and foster a deeper connection with God. They also promote a sense of joy and purpose in life. As Dr. Leaf explains, when we engage in activities that bring us joy or fulfill a purpose larger than ourselves, our brains release dopamine. This feel-good chemical enhances motivation and focus.

I could not contain my excitement when I learned from Dr. Leaf's research that science supports what the Crazy Praise Club has always believed. There is a sense of wonder and exhilaration when we step out of our comfort zones and try something new, and we can present these experiences and joyful emotions as an offering to Jesus in gratitude.

Before we leave the science of the brain, I want to present Dr. Leaf's concept of neuroplasticity, which is the brain's ability to reorganize itself by forming new neural connections. Here are seven key strategies she suggests for

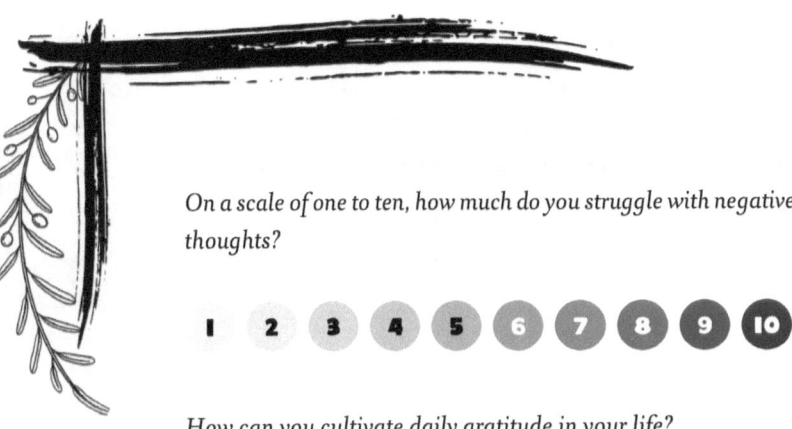

On a scale of one to ten, how much do you struggle with negative thoughts?

1 2 3 4 5 6 7 8 9 10

How can you cultivate daily gratitude in your life?

JOURNAL PROMPT: *When you contemplate the Scripture "Take captive every thought to make it obedient to Christ," what specific areas of your thought life do you think need attention? (Examples might be negative thought patterns, excessive anxiety or worry, a victim mentality, too much focus on external stimuli, etc.)*

JOURNAL PROMPT: *What are some new experiences or spiritual topics you would like to dive into? How will you do that? Don't worry if you don't have many ideas right now—you will have plenty by the time you finish this book. This is just to get you started thinking.*

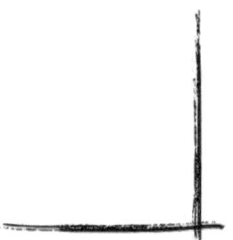

rewiring your brain. Her research suggests that dedicating an average of sixty-three days of consistent practice will solidify these brain-rewiring changes, though the exact timing is unique for each person.

Steps to Rewire Your Brain

1. *Mind Management.* Engage in conscious thinking and self-reflection as you seek Holy Spirit's guidance. This involves monitoring your thoughts, understanding their origins, and managing them effectively. If you have experienced trauma or abuse, you will want to work with a trained professional to help guide you here.

2. *Thought Journaling.* Write down your thoughts to gain clarity and insight. This practice helps in identifying negative thought patterns and re-

placing them with positive ones. As you sense negative patterns creeping up, begin dwelling on the positive ones instead. We have already learned about the power of writing things down from Habakkuk 2:2–3.

3. *Meditation and Mindfulness.* Regular meditation can help reduce stress and improve focus. Mindfulness practices encourage living in the moment and can reshape thought patterns. Worry is simply focusing on issues mostly out of your control and is a waste of time and brain energy. Train yourself to let these thoughts go and trust God with all aspects of your life.

4. *Positive Affirmations.* Use positive self-talk and affirmations to reinforce a positive mindset and challenge negative beliefs. Think about how you can define your identity in Christ and how best to remind yourself of that.

5. *Healthy Lifestyle Choices.* Nutrition, exercise, and sleep play a crucial role in brain health. A balanced diet, regular physical activity, and sufficient rest can enhance cognitive function and will certainly bolster the spiritual journey you are on.

6. *Learning and New Experiences.* Challenge your brain by learning new skills or engaging in activities outside your comfort zone. This stimulates neural growth and strengthens connections.

7. *Visualization Techniques.* Visualizing positive outcomes can help in forming new neural pathways and improving emotional resilience. Imagine Christ being present with you in challenging situations. What would He advise you to do?

By incorporating these practices into your daily routine, you can actively participate in rewiring your brain for better mental health and cognitive function.

IT'S TIME FOR CRAZY PRAISE

Here is an introduction to ways to connect you to your inner creativity. Please don't rush through these creative activities. You can incorporate them into your quiet time or schedule a separate time to do these. Initially, you'll be working alone on the creative-growth activities, but soon you will have opportunities for group interactions.

GOLD
Divinity
Holiness
Glory

PINK
New life
Faith in God
Unconditional
Love

PURPLE
Royalty
Wisdom
Priesthood
Wealth

BROWN
Humility
Devotion
Compassion

WHITE
Fire of God
Passionate
Praise
Deliverance

BLACK
Lack of God's Light
Darkness/Vast
Mourning

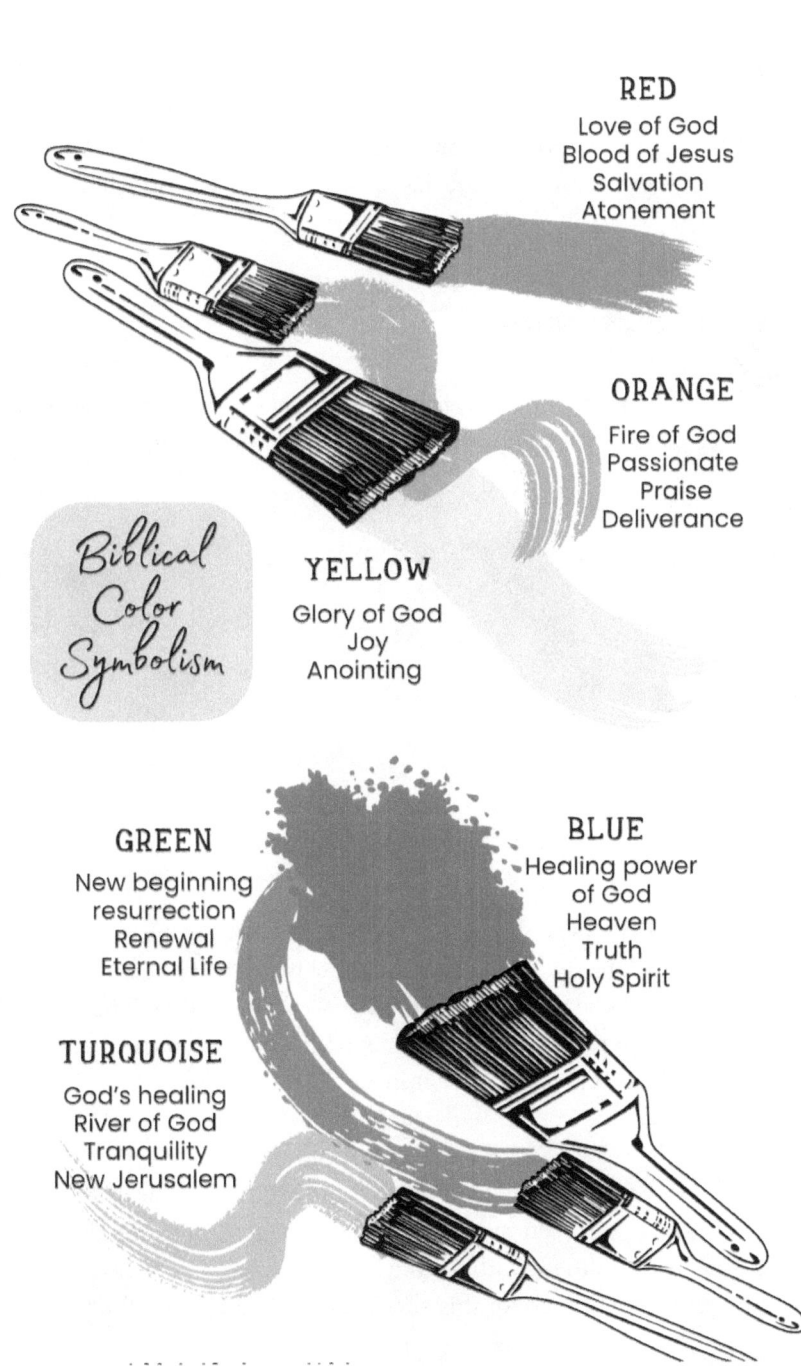

RED
Love of God
Blood of Jesus
Salvation
Atonement

ORANGE
Fire of God
Passionate
Praise
Deliverance

Biblical Color Symbolism

YELLOW
Glory of God
Joy
Anointing

GREEN
New beginning
resurrection
Renewal
Eternal Life

BLUE
Healing power
of God
Heaven
Truth
Holy Spirit

TURQUOISE
God's healing
River of God
Tranquility
New Jerusalem

1. **WORSHIP-MUSIC EXPERIMENT**. Conduct a personal experiment by listening to different forms of worship music and journaling the emotional responses they stir within you. Some suggestions are traditional hymns, classical music such as Handel's Messiah, Contemporary Christian music, instrumental praise music, and gospel. For each, sit quietly and focus on the notes of the music, the words, and what the piece shows you about God.

What music will I listen to this week that is different from my usual selections? After listening, how did that make me feel?

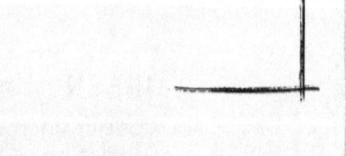

2. **COLOR CHART**. Pull up a color wheel or color chart on your computer. Look at all the ranges of colors and note which you prefer. How do specific colors make you feel? If you have a strong dislike for a color, why is that? You may be inspired to research what emotions specific colors evoke. Note if you feel those things.

3. **BREATH PRAYERS**. Select a short phrase you can repeat with your breath cycle. You may wish to have a few ready for this exercise. With no distractions (you may enjoy sitting outside), sit for fifteen minutes and focus on the breath prayer. It's surprising how challenging it is to concentrate even for this short period. Meditate on the prayer and

see what God speaks to you. Some suggestions for breath prayers are: "Jesus, my peace, I trust You." "Holy Spirit, enter my temple." "Father God, I repent of my sin."

Breath prayers

THEOLOGICAL INSIGHTS
ON PRAISE

We have talked a little about the science of praise. Before we move into transforming our hearts with new practices of praise, it is important to spend a few moments on the historical and theological concept of praise.

Praise is an integral part of the Christian faith. It is not merely an emotional expression but a profound response to the character of God, His deeds, and His presence in our lives. As believers, praise serves as both an individual and communal practice—a means of glorifying God and acknowledging His greatness. In personal worship, praise is a way to express our love, reverence, and gratitude. In community worship, it binds us together as we collectively exalt the name of the Lord. In this chapter, we will delve into the theological underpinnings of praise, exploring its biblical foundations, its relationship with God's nature, and its role in the believer's life.

Definition of Praise

Biblically and theologically, praise is the act of recognizing and declaring the excellence of God. It is not simply an acknowledgment of God's deeds but a deep, heartfelt expression of admiration for His very nature. Praise can take many forms, including words, songs, acts of service, and lives lived in alignment with His will. While praise and worship overlap in many ways, praise differs from worship in that worship involves bowing down and ascribing worth to God, often in response to His presence. Praise, on the other hand, is often spontaneous and celebratory, a declaration of God's greatness. Similarly, thanksgiving focuses on gratitude for what God has done, while praise is broader, encompassing recognition of God's inherent glory in everything.

7 HEBREW WORDS FOR

Praise

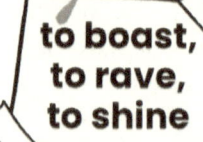

to boast, to rave, to shine

Psalms 149: 3 "Lift up your hands to the holy place."

Halal

Most common Hebrew word for praise

Yadah

Suggest raising the hands as an act of worship and thanksgiving and conveys surrender and reverence

to praise, to give thanks

Psalms 134:2 "Lift up your hands in worship

to bless, to kneel

Psalms 95:6 "Oh come let worship and bow down"

Barak

Implies reverence, humilty and submission through worship

Tehillah

Often refers to a new song or spontaneous Spirit-led worship

to sing a song of praise

Psalms 147:1 "For it is good to sing praises to our God."

to thank, to admit

Psalms 100:4 "Enter his gates with thanksgiving"

Todah

Used to convey praise in difficult circumstances, faith filled offering of gratitude

Zamar

Involves both singing and the use of instruments to worship the Lord

to make music

Psalms 144:9 "I will sing a new song to you God."

to address in a loud tone

Psalms 117:1 "Oh praise the Lord all ye nations."

Shabach

Involves loud triumphant praise, shouting to the Lord with victory

Chapter 3

Biblical Foundations of Praise

Throughout Scripture, praise is a central theme. As you can see by the chart outlining the root words for praise, there are nuances of meaning in the purpose and style of praise we are commanded to pursue. Interestingly, all of these root words (and there even some additional ones!) come into our English bible translation as the word "praise" yet the nuances of meaning God intends are very clear when you contemplate the original language.

In the Psalms, we find an outpouring of praise for God's majesty, His mighty acts of salvation, and His steadfast love. Psalm 150:6 encapsulates the essence of praise: "Let everything that has breath praise the LORD." This command is not restricted to a particular group but extended to all creation. In Hebrews 13:15, the writer encourages believers to "offer to God a sacrifice of praise—the fruit of lips that openly profess His name." Praise is not merely a spontaneous reaction to blessings but a conscious, ongoing expression of faith in God's goodness and greatness.

The Bible emphasizes that praise should be a continual practice—a natural outflow of our relationship with God. It is not merely a ritual or an obligation but a way of life. In both the Old and New Testaments, praise is intertwined with the act of worship, reinforcing the understanding that praising God is essential to the believer's walk.

In our chapter on the brain, we discussed the concept of taking every thought captive for Christ. God would not command us to do something that was impossible to do, so as we adopt the idea of broadening our practice of praise, it is important to also remember that we can glorify God in many different ways, expanding beyond our comfort zones with the goal of glorifying God.

The Nature of God and Praise

Praise is inseparable from a proper understanding of God's nature. As we come to know His holiness, His love, and His sovereignty, our praise becomes a fitting response to who He is. God's holiness—His complete and utter separation from sin—commands reverence. His love, which is unconditional and sacrificial, evokes gratitude and devotion. His sovereignty—His supreme authority over all things—invites awe and admiration. Our understanding of these attributes shapes the way we approach God in praise.

When we praise God for His holiness, we acknowledge His perfection and purity. When we praise Him for His love, we recognize the depth of His grace and mercy. And when we praise Him for His sovereignty, we declare that He alone is worthy of all honor and glory, regardless of our circumstances. When we praise with creativity, we acknowledge His supremely creative nature and His desire to impart that to us.

The Role of Praise in the Life of a Believer

Praise has a profound impact on the believer's life, both inwardly and up-wardly. Inwardly, we have already seen some of that impact on our physical bodies. Emotionally, both honoring and at times breaking with tradition present new opportunities to encounter God. In relation to God, praise strengthens faith by reminding us of God's power and faithfulness. In moments of doubt or trial, praise shifts

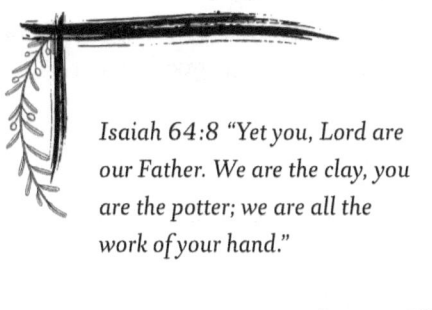

Isaiah 64:8 "Yet you, Lord are our Father. We are the clay, you are the potter; we are all the work of your hand."

our focus from our struggles to God's unchanging character. It reminds us that God is present, that He is at work, and that He is worthy of our trust.

Praise deepens our relationship with God. It is a form of communication—a way of connecting with Him that goes beyond mere words or requests. As we praise God, we acknowledge His presence in our lives, and in turn, our hearts are aligned with His will. Praise, therefore, is not just a response to God's actions but a means of drawing closer to His heart.

If you are a parent, perhaps you have unique ways you connect with each of your children. A friend of mine, who happens to be a potter, was just telling me about doing pottery for the first time with her young granddaughter. She had the girl craft a simple bowl, and together they glazed and fired the piece.

When she placed the finished piece in her granddaughter's hands, the child began to cry. "Gramma," she said, "I just loved feeling the clay in my  hands, making something from it, and then painting it. And look how pretty it came out!" Her granddaughter had a revelation about how pleasurable this process was and was rewarded with a wonderful finished product. It made my friend so happy to guide her granddaughter through this experience, and it gave them a connection that will be ongoing and rewarding for both of them. Similarly, God finds unique ways to connect with His children, and the joy of that connection is deeply rewarding.

Furthermore, praise has the power to transform our perspectives. In the midst of trials, when our vision is clouded by circumstances, praise shifts our attention to God's supremacy. It doesn't diminish the reality of our challenges, but it provides us with the strength to endure by anchoring our hearts in the hope of God's ultimate goodness.

Historical Perspectives on Praise

Over the centuries, various Christian traditions have emphasized the importance of praise in worship. The Catholic Church, with its rich liturgical practices, places a strong emphasis on praise through sacred music and liturgy. The Protestant Reformation, while introducing a more personal and direct approach to worship, still maintained the importance of congregational praise, particularly through hymns and psalms. The Orthodox Church, with its deep connection to the ancient traditions of the early church, continues to emphasize praise through chant and liturgical prayer.

Theologians throughout history have also emphasized the role of praise. Augustine of Hippo wrote extensively on the relationship between worship and praise, emphasizing that true praise comes from a heart transformed by God's grace. John Calvin, while focusing on the sovereignty of God, also recognized the importance of praise as an expression of gratitude and reverence. In modern times, theologians like N. T. Wright have explored the link between the kingdom of God and the act of praise, seeing it as a witness to the world of God's reign.

What is your personal experience with church tradition? Is it new to you, or did you grow up with it? What parts of tradition are important to you, and why?

The Impact of Praise on Community

Praise is not only a personal expression but a communal one. In the body of Christ, communal praise fosters unity and strengthens the bonds between believers. When we come together to praise God, we are reminded that we are part of a larger family, a global community of believers who share the same faith. It is a moment when personal differences are set aside and the focus is solely on God.

Moreover, praise serves as a witness to nonbelievers. When others hear the joyful sound of praise and witness the transformed lives of those who worship, they are given a glimpse of God's glory. As Jesus said in John 17:21 of the unity of believers, "That they may all be one, . . . so that the world may believe that You have sent Me" (ESV). The unity displayed in communal praise becomes a powerful testimony of God's work in the world.

Practical Applications of Praise

Incorporating praise into daily life is essential for maintaining a vibrant relationship with God. Praise can be expressed through music, whether through singing hymns, listening to worship songs, or playing instruments. Personal prayers of praise can be offered throughout the day, even in the midst of routine tasks. Praise can also be expressed through acts of kindness and service, as these actions reflect God's love and goodness.

Gratitude is another form of praise that can be practiced daily. Taking time to reflect on God's blessings, both big and small, and giving thanks are forms of acknowledging His goodness. In moments of difficulty, cultivating a spirit of praise can shift our focus from our circumstances to the faithfulness of God.

Developing a personal practice of praise is important, as it creates a rhythm of connection with God. Some may find it helpful to set aside specific times during the day to focus on praise, while others may express praise spontaneously in response to the beauty of creation, the kindness of others, or moments of personal reflection.

Conclusion

Praise is a vital component of the Christian faith—a theological act that acknowledges God's greatness and goodness. It is both an individual and a communal practice that deepens our relationship with God and strengthens the body of Christ. By understanding the theological foundations of praise, we are better equipped to engage in it with sincerity and reverence. As we grow in our knowledge of God's nature, let our hearts overflow with praise, both in times of joy and in times of trial. May our lives be a continuous offering of praise to the One who is worthy of all honor and glory.

TIME FOR CRAZY PRAISE

1. **SET UP A TIME TO MEET WITH SOMEONE YOU KNOW WHO GOES TO A DIFFERENT CHURCH.** Tell them you want to better understand some of the historical context of their praise practices. Go the meeting full of curiosity and seeking to truly understand the roots of their faith.

2. **VISIT A MUSEUM OR EXHIBITION BUILT AROUND THE IDEA OF THE HISTORY OF RELIGION, OR SOMETHING TO DO WITH RELIGIOUS EXPERIENCES.** Hone in on a handful of items that are of particular interest, and think and pray about the connection between the biblical perspective on faith and this historical presentation. Journal about what you learn, then contemplate how that might speak into your own life.

3. **WHICH BIBLICAL CHARACTERS DO YOU THINK PARTICULARLY EMBODY PRAISE, AND WHY?** Do a mini Bible study about how different people in the Bible expressed their praise. Push yourself to think beyond the obvious choices. Gather a small group of friends to study together and see what you can discover.

BIBLICAL THEMES, IDEAS, OR CHARACTERS
I WANT TO EXPLORE

Here's how I'll explore this topic

☐ *Watch online content*
☐ *Read a book or article*
☐ *Go to an exhibition*
☐ *Talk with pastors or subject matter experts*
☐ *Do a bible study either alone or with a group*
☐ *Complete a related art project or drawing*
☐ *Research root words*
☐ *Other:_____*

BALANCING TRADITION AND NEW EXPRESSIONS

Our spiritual practices are in many ways a reflection of the traditions we belong to. Our traditions can be so important to us, as they give us a sense of identity and connect us with our roots. They can be a comfort and a safe place because of their predictability. While we value our traditions, trying new things brings about spiritual growth, as we have learned. New approaches to worship and praise that are not familiar and challenge us to go beyond or outside of our traditions can be a great tool for building a new level of intimacy with God.

Our challenge here is to seek God in new ways. That's not to say we need to throw out the old ways but that we are intentional about our practices. It is important to honor our roots and where we are coming from spiritually. At the same time, it is possible to embrace new practices of praise. It's not either-or.

There are some critical considerations to think about as we contemplate our current practices. We don't want to do things by rote. Instead, we need to think about the underlying meaning of our traditions and approach them anew. It's worth spending some time considering a different paradigm.

Sadly, for some of us, our spiritual traditions actually serve to stifle our growth. Maybe we need to break free from just going through the motions of our old-school ways of worship that have become empty and lost their meaning for us. In those cases, those practices are like outdated fashion trends that don't quite fit any more—they're like trying to dance in a suit of armor at a beach party! Rote rituals can be as stifling as wearing a hat two sizes too small on a sunny day, squishing our creativity and blocking the sunshine of our connection with the divine. For those questioning the relevance of tradition, it may be time to consider ditching the spiritual hand-me-downs and stepping into fresh, comfy sneakers that let us groove freely in our unique God-connection dance.

10 FACTS ABOUT COMMUNION

Prayerfully think about communion with a fresh perspective. There is room to jot down some notes about your thoughts at the end of each prompt.

1. Communion was instituted by Jesus. It began at the Last Supper (Matt 26:26-28) as a way for believers to remember Christ's sacrifice. What do you think your reaction would be if you were at a meal with Christ and he took the actions that have become communion?

2. Symbolic elements. The bread symbolizes Jesus' body, and the wine symbolizes his blood shed for forgiveness. How can you contemplate Jesus when partaking of the bread and juice?

3. Old Testament foreshadowing. Communion is rooted in Passover. Jesus is the ultimate Passover Lamb (1 Cor 5:7). Research some passages in scripture that foretell Christ's sacrifice and make note of your reactions here.

4. It proclaims the Gospel. 1 Corinthians 11:26 says that taking communion declares Christ's death until He returns. What are your thoughts about Christ's return?

5. It's a covenant renewal. The cup represents the new covenant in Jesus' blood (Luke 22: 20), signifying restored relationship with God. What does the idea of "covenant" represent for you?

6. Unity in the body. Communion represents the spiritual unity of all believers (I Cor 10:17). Describe a time when corporate communion was particularly meaningful for you.

7. Early Christians were persecuted over it. Romans misunderstood the language around communion and accused Christians of cannibalism. If you were to be persecuted for taking communion, would you still do it? Why or why not?

8. It can be misused. Paul warns in 1 Cor 11: 27030 about taking communion in an unworthy manner, pointing to its holiness. What things in your own life might inhibit you from taking communion?

9. Practiced differently across denominations. Protestants believe in communion as a symbolic memorial, whereas Catholics take a transubstantiation view. What is your understanding of the difference?

10. Time for healing and reflection. Communion is a moment for repentance, restoration and spiritual renewal. Recall some times when taking communion represented repentance, restoration or spiritual renewal for you.

For those who flourish in the worship traditions you love, the invitation still stands to enhance your worship life by adding in new approaches. The degree to which you do this is entirely up to you. It's like going swimming in the ocean—some prefer to wade, some prefer to go in up to their knees, and others are looking for a full swim. Whatever your preference, if you are chasing a joyful heart, I invite you to push yourself a bit to catch it!

Tradition vs. Connection

Reflect on the traditions of your church or faith community. Are they enhancing your connection with God or hindering it? Are there any practices that feel stale or irrelevant to you? It is important to honor and respect traditions, but remember that your worship should always lead you closer to God.

Sometimes, we go through the motions of something without truly pondering its depth of meaning. Take time to stop and consider how these traditions started and how they are intended to bring you closer to God. Recently, I spent time educating myself on the sacrament of Communion. What does it mean? What does Jesus say about it? What about the condition of my heart when I take Communion? This study and contemplation caused me to become very emotional about the act of Communion and view it in a completely fresh light. Learning and opening the door to new approaches to this sacred practice led to a deeper connection with God.

Here is a graphic with 10 facts about communion. You may already be familiar with most of these, but I invite you to look at this with fresh eyes. Prayerfully consider the deep symbolism Jesus was explaining to us, especially in light of the fact that He knew He was soon going to death for us. Think about each of these ten facts in light of Christ's sacrifice for you. As you meditate on the act of communion, consider preparing a communion for your family, small group or friends. Then partake of communion in a new place – perhaps outside in a park, in someone's home, at a historic location or a difference church or chapel than usual. Be reverent as you partake, and ask Jesus to draw near to you in a new way through this act of surrender to Christ.

Embrace Diversity

Step outside your own tradition by exploring different forms of worship from various cultures and denominations that have different traditions from yours.

Attend services or events of other faith communities and embrace the diversity of expressions in worship. This can broaden your perspective and help you connect with God in new ways. One thing I found particularly enlightening was talking with friends who have done mission trips to other countries. They shared about the different ways other cultures honor and love God and how profound their devotion to Him can be. Their stories deeply moved me and showed me a great deal about the heart of God.

A particular passion of mine, and one I recommend to you if you have the ability to access it, is to connect with Jewish ministries. We have a great one in Atlanta—Light of Messiah Ministries. It is run by people who were raised in the Jewish faith or who have lived in Isreal for a time, and they specifically minister to Jews here and in Isreal. They do a great job of bridging the gap of knowledge we Gentile

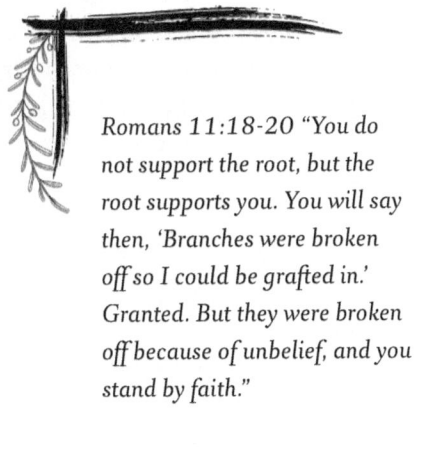

Romans 11:18-20 "You do not support the root, but the root supports you. You will say then, 'Branches were broken off so I could be grafted in.' Granted. But they were broken off because of unbelief, and you stand by faith."

Christians can have about why God loves these people so much and why it's so important to support them. I have learned so much about my own faith and especially how best to share the Lord with Jewish friends. If you don't have access to attend live social events, connect online with one or more of these ministries, sign up for their newsletters, and invite them to share with your group either in person or remotely.

There may be other peoples or regions that you are particularly interested in. Some of my friends are especially interested in spreading the gospel in the 10-40 Window, which is a region where many unreached people groups live. It is very dangerous to enter these countries because you can be jailed, and even tortured, for being a Christian. It's hard to comprehend that there are so many areas of the world where there is no freedom of religion and Christians are actively persecuted. Embracing these cultures and peoples is definitely a form of praise!

Personalization

Consider ways to personalize your own worship experience so it is more meaningful to you—maybe through art, dance, writing, contemplative communion or other creative means. Perhaps it is worship in a natural setting. Maybe it takes the form of Bible word studies. Think about what speaks to your heart and soul and stirs you deeply in your faith walk. Don't be afraid to incorporate these elements into your personal time with God.

Although highly personal, worship can also involve other people. I often host small dinner parties where we have a theme on which we all share. This might be a personal testimony about a struggle, a time when God helped us overcome pain, a profound gratitude session, or sharing family holiday traditions. These get-togethers deepen our sense of relationship to both Jesus and one another.

Musical Interlude

Think about some memories you have of certain songs. Do you have that one song that immediately takes you back to high school every time you hear it? A falling-in-love or break-up song may immediately evoke certain feelings when you listen to it—no crying in the car!

There is a vast library of music that helps connect us to God. For some, it is traditional hymns. Perhaps you enjoy the worship music of past decades. The early Contemporary Christian singers resonate with me because that's what we listened to in youth group and my early concerts. They were guideposts for my early formative years in my faith. Sometimes, even an instrumental version of an old favorite can cause you to appreciate it anew. As we step beyond our traditions, we can incorporate music into the transformative journey toward finding new levels of intimacy with God through our praise.

Recently, I listened to a piano version of "Turn Your Eyes upon Jesus." I have heard and sung this song thousands of times, but hearing it in this new, unique arrangement was incredibly moving. Likewise, I have some friends who got married, and the bride walked down the aisle to a classical-guitar version of "As the Deer." I was weeping with emotion at the beauty of the song and the bride! In fact, after the ceremony, the bride told me, "I was fine until I saw you crying, then I immediately started crying as well!"

Music ignites areas of the brain completely distinct from reading or speaking, making it beneficial to harness this powerful tool when we praise. Just as there are different neural pathways for color, shape, and textures (thus the term "visual learner"), so there are different pathways for sound and music. Here is just one example of the impact music can have.

Consider this story recounted by Barbara Wheeler in her book *The Music Therapy Primer*. A young boy named Daniel, who was diagnosed with autism, was primarily nonverbal. His family struggled to find ways to communicate with him until they noticed his love of music. They engaged him with music-therapy sessions. In these sessions, Daniel would respond to melodies and engage with instruments in ways that expressed his feelings and desires. One poignant moment came when Daniel created a song about his daily routine. He began to hum and clap to indicate he wanted to communicate, perhaps feeling happy or wanting to play.

Through music, Daniel began to connect with his family and therapist. His ability to express himself grew. Though he never gained command of language skills, Daniel was able to significantly expand his world and relationships by communicating through music.*

Listening Challenge

Experiment with incorporating listening to music in a new way into your transformative praise journey. Select songs from some or all of the following genres, and choose at least three songs per genre. Listen to the songs at least three times and ask yourself, "Is God speaking to me through these words? If so, what is He saying? In what ways does the music move me? How is this music praiseworthy and praise-enhancing?"

As you make a playlist of songs from the following list of musical categories, you might also enjoy listening to the musical artists explain how and why they wrote their songs. I recently heard the lyricist for "Let Faith Arise" explain how he wrote it after a debilitating season of anxiety in which he couldn't even get out of bed. This gave me a new appreciation for the song, and I steeped myself in the song for several days.

---

* Barbara L. Wheeler, *The Music Therapy Primer* (Silver Spring, MD: American Music Therapy Association, 2015).

 Here are some categories of music to explore, along with a few suggested artists:

- *Contemporary Christian Music.* Artist suggestions: Tauren Wells, Lauren Daigle, Casting Crowns
- *Gospel.* Artist suggestions: Kirk Franklin, Yolanda Adams, Tamela Mann
- *Worship Music, Current.* Artist suggestions: Chris Tomlin, Matthew Maher, Matt Redman
- *Christian Rock.* Artist suggestions: Switchfoot, Skillet, Red
- *Christian Hip-Hop.* Artist suggestions: TobyMac, Lecrae, Andy Mineo
- *Christian Pop.* Artist suggestions: For King and Country, Phil Wickham, Jeremy Camp, Francesca Battistelli
- *Traditional Hymns:* "How Great Thou Art," "It Is Well with My Soul," "Crown Him with Many Crowns." Artist suggestions: Mahalia Jackson, the Brooklyn Tabernacle Choir, CeCe Winans
- *Contemporary Worship.* Artist suggestions: Vineyard Church, Hosanna Music, Maranatha! Music, Hillsong, Don Moen
- *Early Christian-Radio Music.* Artist suggestions: Keith Green, Amy Grant, Michael W. Smith, Randy Stonehill, Phil Keaggy
- *Messianic Jewish Music.* Artist suggestions: Lamb, Joshua Aaron, Paul Wilbur, Marty Goetz, Shilo Ben Hod, Liberated Wailing Wall

Research the origins of the artists you select to make sure you are in alignment with their doctrine and faith base. Go on YouTube and type in the song or artist title, then see what reviews come up from teachers you respect. Watch those videos and see if you agree.

Letting Go of Fear

Sometimes, we hold on to traditions out of fear—fear of change, judgment, or not being good enough. But know that breaking free from these fears can open new avenues for connection with God. Trust in His love and His desire for an authentic relationship with you. As you consider breaking free from traditions that do not serve you in your pursuit of authentic praise, is God bringing anything to the forefront that you want to ask Him about? What would you like to delve into more deeply?

The Importance of Community

From the very beginning, God emphasized community. He Himself exists in community as a Trinity—three together in one. In the lush, vibrant garden of Eden, He declared that it was not good for Adam to be alone (Genesis 2:18). Throughout the pages of the Bible, we witness how God specifically crafted us for fellowship with one another. The Son of God, Jesus Christ, exemplified this divine design by surrounding Himself with a diverse and devoted community of disciples. His earthly ministry was characterized by constant engagement with people from all walks of life, regardless of social status or background.

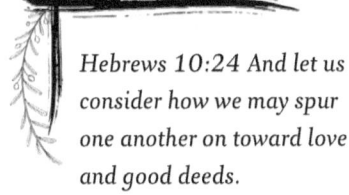

Hebrews 10:24 And let us consider how we may spur one another on toward love and good deeds.

The community is vital to connecting with God in worship. When we unite as a body of believers, we can encourage and support one another on our faith journeys. We can learn from each other's experiences, share our struggles and triumphs, and grow in our relationship with God. As much as I love preparing materials and content around a topic, it becomes so much better when I teach or share it with a group and add all their insights to my understanding. It truly comes alive!

The community also holds us accountable for living out our faith. Through fellowship and accountability, we can spur each other on to love and good deeds (Hebrews 10:24). This is especially important for those who may struggle with their faith or feel disconnected from God. Having a supportive community can bring them back into alignment with Him. Even if you are an introvert or prefer alone time, it's important to connect with others in some way.

Fostering Unity in Worship

In today's world of division, Christians foster unity within their communities through worship. Worship is a unifying act that transcends differences in race, culture, socio-economic status, and political views. As followers of Christ, we are called to love one another as He loves us (John 13:34). By coming together in worship despite our differences, we demonstrate this love to the world.

One way to foster unity in worship is to focus on our shared beliefs and values rather than our differences, which are often a matter of personal preference. Every form of prayer is valuable as long as we give all glory to Jesus. Paul even cautions us in 2 Corinthians not to focus on doctrinal differences but on our unity in Christ.

Particularly since Covid, it can be tempting to exclusively stream pastors or services we enjoy. It is vital that we meet together in person and build relationships as well as worship corporately. You can stream as an extension of your in-person connection, but I caution you against the isolation that exclusively streaming can bring. It is important to contribute and serve within a body of believers.

So, let's broaden our perspectives and focus on praising the name of Jesus!

IT'S TIME FOR CRAZY PRAISE

Imagine your faith journey as a path through a vast and enchanting forest. Many have traveled well-worn trails that provide a sense of familiarity and security. But what about the untouched paths that veer off into the unknown? They might lead you to hidden clearings filled with wildflowers and bird songs or tranquil streams reflecting the sky's boundless beauty. Each person's journey is unique, and you can grow when you courageously forge your own path.

What might be some new avenues of praise that genuinely resonate with your soul? In the chapters ahead, we will experiment with different forms of prayer, explore diverse spiritual practices, and seek out communities that embrace a variety of expressions of faith. When we are willing to reexamine our traditions and step into new experiences of praise, we open ourselves up to a deeper, more authentic connection with the divine.

Remember, your spiritual journey is just that—yours. So, embrace the adventure and let your faith flourish in ways that are truly meaningful to you.

"For freedom Christ has set us free; stand firm therefore, and do not submit again to a yoke of slavery" (Galatians 5:1 ESV).

In what ways do you see trying new forms of worship as an expression of your spiritual freedom?

"Being confident of this, that He who began a good work in you will carry it on to completion until the day of Christ Jesus" (Philippians 1:6).

How do you view praise in relation to the "good work" Jesus is doing in you?

"He replied, 'Isaiah was right when he prophesied about you hypocrites; as it is written: "These people honor Me with their lips, but their hearts are far from Me. They worship Me in vain; their teachings are merely human rules." You have let go of the commands of God and are holding on to human traditions." (Mark 7:6−8).

What role do your traditions of worship play in your practice of praise? How can you hold on to the traditions you find fulfilling and embrace new avenues of praise?

INTERACTIVE WORSHIP ACTIVITIES

Unleashing Your God-Given Potential

We have laid the groundwork for understanding how praise practices are rooted in well-worn pathways within the brain. We looked at the theology of praise. Then, in the last chapter, we examined the role tradition can play in praise. That is a beginning, but it is not where we end.

Now, I invite you to reach for more. Here you will find ways to seek greater intimacy and creative ways to know God, all through the power of praise. New areas of your brain will light up as you take every thought captive for Christ. You may have the opportunity to connect with fellow believers who share your interests as you broaden your horizons into new territory. Or, if you press into praise with the people with whom you currently do life, you'll feel those bonds getting stronger.

As you draw closer to God through praise, there are three ways it will impact your walk with Him:

1. *Reflect Inward.* You will reflect on yourself—your strengths and weaknesses, your passions, and your desires. God speaks through all of these. Ask God to reveal how He has specifically gifted you and how you can use those gifts for His glory.

2. *Know Jesus Upward.* As you deepen your relationship with Christ, you will better understand His heart and plans for your life. Allow Him to shape and guide you as you seek to fulfill your purpose.

3. *Expand Outward.* You will step out of your comfort zone and be open to new opportunities to interact with others that align with your gifts and passions. Whether leading, serving, teaching, or discipling, look for ways to use your gifts to bless others.

REFLECT *inward*

Reflect on yourself—your strengths and weaknesses, your passions, and your desires. God speaks through all of these. Ask God to reveal how He has specifically gifted you and how you can use those gifts for His glory.

As you deepen your relationship with Christ, you will better understand His heart and plans for your life. Allow Him to shape and guide you as you seek to fulfill your purpose.

KNOW JESUS *upward*

EXPAND *outward*

Step out of your comfort zone and be open to new opportunities to interact with others that align with your gifts and passions. Whether leading, serving, teaching, or discipling, look for ways to use your gifts to bless others.

As you delve into the heart of this chapter, a treasure trove of innovative ideas unfolds. It offers a transformative approach to praise and worship that will push you in new directions. It beckons you to embark on a journey of active participation, where worship becomes a dynamic interplay between the finite and the infinite, the earthly and the divine.

Imagine yourself in a sanctuary, not of physical confines but of the soul, where the walls echo with the rhythm of your heartbeat and the ceiling stretches to embrace the infinite sky. Here, the boundaries between the seen and unseen blur. The worship activities presented in this chapter are offered as your compass in that sanctuary, guiding you toward a deeper connection with God the Father, Jesus, and the Holy Spirit. Importantly, you are invited to open your heart and mind to possibilities you may not have considered before. Enter into a process of discovery that has no end.

When I moved into my home about four years ago, I began anchoring the space with key items. I chose flooring I loved, changed paint colors in certain rooms, and set up some anchoring furniture. But over the past four years, I have added many new items that make me more comfortable in my space. Recently, for example, I changed several light fixtures.

In my office, I placed a crystal chandelier with a clear fan that comes out on cue (one word—menopause!). I ordered a custom blind and redid the closet to function as an office-supply space. After adding a blue desk, a repurposed credenza, and an inexpensive bookshelf, my dream office is now where I love being creative and productive. I finished it with some pottery and a head vase friends gifted me. I'm writing this book here right now! Exploring how I wanted to set up this space in a way that appeals to my senses and activates my creativity has changed my life, but it has been a process. I love my space and being here, and it will forever evolve. It is a space dedicated to praising God in the various ways the Lord has given me to do that.

Your spiritual worship space is similar. As you open your heart to experiencing the Creator in new ways, you will furnish that sacred sanctuary of praise in ways that serve your unique, ever-evolving life of worship. There is no telling what you may discover about yourself. This chapter is intended as a beacon, illuminating a path that invites you to embrace worship as a holistic experience. It encourages you to explore your faith through movement, reflection, and creative expression. All your gestures, thoughts, emotions, and deeds can be part of bringing you closer to the heart of God. Prepare to embark on a sacred adventure where worship becomes the bridge between the body, mind, and spirit and every interaction with the divine leaves an indelible mark on your soul.

Praise is a powerful catalyst for transformation—a divine alchemy that transforms our hearts from merely existing to becoming vibrant expressions of joy and gratitude. As we engage in interactive praise activities, we will reflect on how praise leads us on a journey of inward growth, upward connection to Jesus, and outward service to others.

In the Scriptures, we find compelling examples of individuals who embraced radical praise, fundamentally changing their lives and the lives of those around them. David, the shepherd boy who became a king, exemplified this beautifully. Despite facing numerous trials, his heart overflowed with praise. He danced before the Lord with abandon, declaring, "I will praise You, O LORD, with my whole heart" (Psalm 9:1 NKJV). His radical praise deepened his relationship with God and inspired a nation to worship. The result? An enduring legacy of faith and a psalm-filled heart that continues to resonate through the generations.

Similarly, Mary, the mother of Jesus, offered an extraordinary expression of praise when she visited her cousin Elizabeth. Filled with the Holy Spirit, she proclaimed, "My soul magnifies the Lord, and my spirit rejoices in God my Savior" (Luke 1:46–47 ESV). Her humble yet profound acknowledgment of God's greatness transformed her circumstances and empowered her to embrace her pivotal role in salvation history. Her praise echoed not just in her life but in the lives of countless believers who would come after her.

Then, as we go on to explore the concept of interactive praise, we can draw inspiration from biblical examples and enjoy expanding the experiences to a broader community of believers.

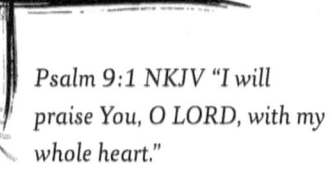

Psalm 9:1 NKJV "I will praise You, O LORD, with my whole heart."

Now we will dive into some new pathways for praise. Here are seven immersive worship-experience categories to enrich your spiritual journey. Try a few different praise experiences from within each category. Each new challenge will ignite new areas of your brain and help you practice taking every thought captive for Christ. As you unleash your God-given potential, remember your goal. You want to grow in intimacy with God and use what He has given you to serve others and bring glory to His name. Stay humble, stay connected to Christ, and watch Him do amazing things through you.

1. *Artistic Expression.* Create an art project that reflects your praise. Use paints, clay, or collage materials to express your gratitude and worship. Or, craft a piece of jewelry or make a journal. Host an art night with friends where everyone creates something representing their relationship with God. It is often helpful to start with a particular word, theme, or color—for example, start with your focus word for the year.

In chapter 1, we learned how interaction with colors, materials, sounds, and words causes new parts of our brain to light up. As a writer, I especially respond to guided journaling practices. Lately, I have been doing that on blank paper and then using colored markers or pencils to expand upon the ideas. There are also journaling and coloring Bibles especially designed for this. They represent an entirely new way to interact with God's Word. I focus on one word or theme and think about it in order to allow new ideas to be revealed to me.

Consider this case study directly from the Word of God in which tangible objects and craftsmanship connected people with God and deepened their praise: as we look at the ark of the covenant in the Old Testament, we see how each meticulously crafted element was a love letter to God and can inspire us to bring our craftsmanship into our worship practices.

The ark of the covenant was a sacred object God commanded Moses to make as the seat in the holy of holies where His presence would come and dwell with His people. It was made according to specific instructions given by God to Moses (Exodus 25:10–22) and served as a physical representation of the perfect heavenly things not made with human hands. The intricate design and materials used in crafting the ark held deep spiritual significance.

The lid of the ark was the mercy seat, which was made of pure gold and adorned with cherubim on either end (Exodus 25:17–22). This represented God's throne and signified His authority over all things. The cherubim were symbolic guardians, reflecting God's protection over His holiness and over His people.

The ark was made of acacia wood overlaid with gold inside and out. This combination represented divinity and humanity in perfect harmony. The rings attached to the sides allowed it to be transported by poles, emphasizing its sacredness and untouchable nature.

The Tabernacle

As you look at this illustration, observe the range and types of artisan handiwork that went into this place to worship God. They include metal work, fabric, carpenters and wood cutters, tent makers, gold and bronze inlay artists, candlmakers, gemstone cutters and bakers. Any talent can be offered to God as a form of praise, because He gave it to each person!

The Holy of Holies

The Ark of the Covenant

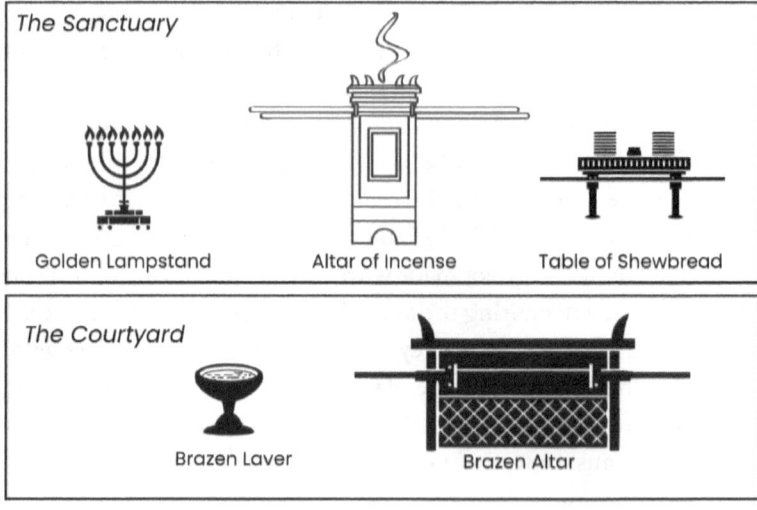

The Sanctuary

Golden Lampstand   Altar of Incense   Table of Shewbread

The Courtyard

Brazen Laver   Brazen Altar

Outer Courtyard

Entrance and Curtain Fence   The Tabernacle

The ark's contents were also significant. It contained three objects: Aaron's staff, a jar of manna, and the stone tablets inscribed with the Ten Commandments (Hebrews 9:4). These items represented Israel's past, present, and future relationship with God.

The meticulous attention paid to every detail in creating this object reflects its importance and the ancient Israelites' deep love and reverence for God. It served as a reminder that God is holy, mighty, just, loving, and ever-present among His people.

Just as the ark of the covenant shows how ancient artisans worshipped God with their workmanship, so our artistic expressions can serve as a love letter of praise to our Creator. No matter your gifting and talent, your sacred pathway, or your personality, use that to express your love to Jesus. Remember, you are taking every thought captive for Christ when you worship in innovative ways.

Art as a form of worship is a great place to begin exploration of new and innovative praise opportunities. Then, we'll move into some other ideas for creative praise. Even if you've done some of these before, take the time to explore them again in light of what you have learned in this book. View each experience as a way to grow in your adoration of God.

Finding Healing through Art

Art has been used throughout history for expression, communication, and documentation. But beyond its beauty, the very act of creating has potential for bringing about healing. Studies have shown that creative activities can reduce stress, increase self-awareness and mindfulness, and improve overall mental health.

Art can be a powerful tool for discovery in our spiritual journey. Just as King David expressed his emotions through songwriting and playing music (Psalm 40:3), we, too, can use artistic outlets to connect with God on a deeper level.

1. The Creative Process as Therapy

Art involves using our hands, minds, and hearts to create something new. This process can be incredibly therapeutic, allowing us to express ourselves in unique ways that may be difficult to express through words alone.

Research has shown that engaging in the creative process increases dopamine levels in the brain, which play a role in motivation, pleasure, and reward. This surge of dopamine can produce joy and satisfaction as we see our ideas come to life through art.

Furthermore, creating art allows us to tap into our subconscious and bring up buried emotions or thoughts. Focusing on the task quiets our inner critic, allowing for more introspection and self-reflection. This can lead to a better understanding of ourselves and even promote healing from past traumas or emotional wounds.

Consider what kinds of art might speak to you, and take a broad definition of art, as we explored in the Ark of the Covenant. It may be some combination of skilled trade, craft, design, using implements like brushes or pens, working with precious metals or gems - take a broad definition of how you can worship through the artistic expression God built into you.

2. Outdoor Activities. Engaging with nature as a form of worship is a powerful and meaningful way to connect with God. In today's fast-paced, technology-driven world, neglecting the beauty and wonder of the natural world around us can be easy. However, intentionally engaging with nature can bring us closer to God and remind us of His power, creativity, and love for us.

Plan an Outdoor Excursion

Going on an outdoor excursion is a straightforward way to engage with nature as worship. This could include hiking, bike riding, picnicking in the park, or walking in your neighborhood. The key is intentionally immersing yourself in nature and focusing on your surroundings.

As you spend time outdoors, notice the beauty around you. Pay attention to your surroundings' colors, textures, sounds, and smells. Admire the intricate details of a flower or the patterns in a tree's bark. Be fully present in the moment and allow yourself to be amazed by God's creation.

Praise God for His Handiwork

While engaging with nature, take time to praise God for His handiwork. Psalm 19:1 says, "The heavens declare the glory of God; the skies proclaim the work of His hands." As we marvel at the wonders of nature around us, we are reminded that all creation testifies to God's greatness.

You can praise God through prayer or by singing worship songs surrounded by nature. You can also read passages from Scripture that speak about God's creation, such as Psalm 104 or Job 38–41.

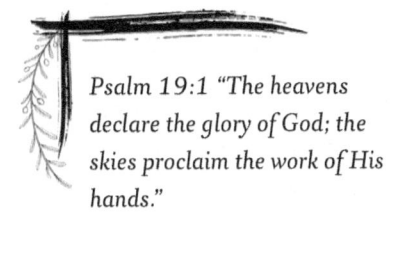

Psalm 19:1 "The heavens declare the glory of God; the skies proclaim the work of His hands."

It is easy to offer cursory praise when you see something beautiful but quickly move on without truly appreciating it. Instead, make an effort to study and understand what you are seeing. Ask questions like:

- How did this come to be?
- What purpose does it serve?
- How do the intricate details reveal a characteristic of God to me?
- What is God saying to me through this detail of creation?

The waves on the beach and the stars in the sky move me. When I consider them, they remind me of my mortality and God's infinite greatness. I contemplate my insignificance in the grand scheme of humanity. Yet despite my smallness, God deeply loves and care for me—just little insignificant me on the edge of this vast ocean.

3. Prayer Walk. One powerful way to engage with nature as worship is to do a prayer walk in your neighborhood or community. This walk can be done individually or in a group. The purpose is to pray intentionally for the people and places you encounter. Here's how to get started:

Choose a Route

The first step in organizing a prayer walk is to choose a route. You can choose your neighborhood, a nearby park, or any other area you feel led to pray for. You can plan your route so you know where you will be walking and can easily navigate the area.

During the holidays, I go on a "Gift Walk" where I hand out gift bags with candy and bookmarks to friends in a specific neighborhood. The results are always unexpected. Before moving on from each recipient, I ask if I can pray with or for them. I have rarely been turned down when offering prayer!

Chapter 5

Pray for Guidance

Before embarking on your prayer walk, take time to pray for guidance. Ask God to open your eyes and heart to His leading as you walk through the community. You may also want to pray specifically for the people and places you will encounter and ask God to reveal any specific needs or areas He wants you to focus on.

Let Your Feet Be Your Testimony

As you begin your prayer walk, let your feet be your testimony. Let each step serve as worship and intercession for those around you. Pray silently or aloud as you feel led, lifting prayers for individuals, homes, businesses, schools, and other areas that catch your attention.

Acknowledge God's Presence

Remember to acknowledge God's presence in every corner of your surroundings as you continue your prayer walk. Psalm 139:7–10 says, "Where shall I go from Your Spirit? Or where shall I flee from Your presence? If I ascend to heaven, You are there! If I make my bed in Sheol [the grave!], You are there! If I take the wings of the morning and dwell in the uttermost parts of the sea, even there Your hand shall lead me" (ESV).

Be aware that God is with you on this journey, and allow His presence to guide your prayers.

Psalm 139:7-8 "Where can I go from your Spirit? Where can I flee from your presence? If I go up to the heavens, you are there; if I make my bed in the depths, you are there."

4. *Studying and Learning a New Activity.* Explore a new skill or hobby that you can dedicate to God. Whether you learn an instrument, garden, or cook, infuse your practice with praise. Share your journey with others, allowing your passion to inspire their hearts toward worship.

A few years ago, I discovered an unknown passion when I began painting furniture as a hobby. My first creation was a table my neighbor and his daughter had crafted that they no longer wanted. The challenge was that the table was goldenrod, and my house was decorated with blue, ivory, and sage green. I decided to paint the golden color a soft blue.

Once the paint was on, I distressed the piece, then adding layers of gray glaze because it needed depth. I watched YouTube videos and took several in-person classes. The best part was I discovered a friend was very into furniture painting, and we bonded and expanded our friendship over this shared hobby. When I completed my first project, I was so excited that God had shown me an aspect of my creativity I never knew I would love so much. Throughout the process, I marveled at how the layers of color were like the many layers of God, nuanced and evoking a deeply emotional response.

I pray you will discover new ways to praise God and learn more about yourself. A few years later, I continue to embrace painting and have several pieces displayed in my home. I have begun sharing this hobby with friends through gifting them with pieces, often incorporating symbols or Scripture references that reflect my attitude of praise as I created the piece.

5. *Christian Events.* Attending Christian events is a great way to enhance your spiritual journey and grow closer to God. It allows you to connect with like-minded believers, learn more about your faith, and deepen your understanding of God's love and purpose for your life. However, with so many events available, choosing the ones that will genuinely impact your journey can be overwhelming. Here are some guidelines for choosing meaningful Christian events.

Pray for Guidance

Before deciding on which event to attend, take some time to pray and ask God for guidance. Ask Him to lead you to the right event to help you grow your relationship with Him. Surrender your plans and preferences to Him, and trust He will guide you in the right direction.

One area God has ignited within me is learning more about Judaism. I have connected with some local ministries that work exclusively with Orthodox Jews and have a boots-on-the-ground ministry in Israel. I attend several events, subscribe to their newsletter and online materials, and support them financially. This has opened up an entirely new aspect of my faith and made me much more aware of what should be a vitally important focus area for all Christians.

Know Your Interests and Needs

Consider topics, interests, events, or areas of your faith you want to focus on or learn more about. Are there specific struggles or challenges you are facing that you want to address? Knowing your interests and needs will help you narrow down the type of event most beneficial for you.

Research Different Events

Take some time to research different Christian events in your area or online. Look at their websites or social media pages to better understand the topics they cover, the speakers or presenters involved, and their overall mission and values.

Consider the Format

Christian events can take various forms, such as conferences, seminars, workshops, and retreats. Look at the best format for you based on your interests, schedule, and budget.

Seek Recommendations from Others

Ask friends, family members, or church leaders for recommendations based on their experiences attending Christian events. They can suggest an event that perfectly matches your needs.

Event Challenge

Research and locate two Christian events you would like to attend this year. You may want to recruit a spouse or friend to go with you. The only requirement is to choose events you have never attended and push yourself into new territory. A women's conference, Christian concert, lecture, or museum exhibition might be a good place to start.

7 Pillars of Self Care

REST
"be still and know"
Ps. 46:10

MOVEMENT
"In Him we live and move
and have our being."
Acts 17:28

NOURISHMENT
"Your body is a temple of
the Holy Spirit."
1 Cor 6:19

JOY AND CREATIVITY
"The joy of the lord."
Neh. 8:10

BOUNDARIES
"Let your 'yes' be 'yes'."
Matt. 5:37

COMMUNITY
"Encourage one
another in love."
1 Thess 5:11

PRAYER AND REFLECTION
"Cast your cares on Him."
1 Peter 5:7

6. *Praise through Health.* As Christians, we often focus on serving and caring for others. While this is essential to our faith, we sometimes neglect our own health and well-being. However, I have learned that taking care of ourselves is necessary to effectively serve others and fulfill God's purpose for our lives.

My Personal Health Journey

Let me share a bit about my health journey and how I praise the Lord through it. I have struggled with yo-yo dieting and fad diets for most of my life. After my journey through a hysterectomy and menopause, I gained over seventy pounds and was diagnosed with severe joint inflammation. This was a wake-up call for me, as I had a family history of diabetes and knew I needed to make some changes.

I tried many different diets and weight-loss programs over the years, but nothing seemed to stick. Then, in 2023, I hit rock bottom regarding my physical health. I was diagnosed with severe arthritis and high blood pressure and put on numerous medications. Honestly, I could barely walk—I was in so much pain. My body was inflamed, I wasn't sleeping, and I felt terrible all the time.

But during this low point, God spoke to me about the importance of caring for my body as His temple. He showed me that I needed to prioritize my health to continue serving Him and fulfilling His purpose for my life. I asked Him to guide me to the right resources, educated myself, and wrote out a plan. He guided me on my journey and brought people into my life to help me.

I started making changes. I adopted an intermittent-fasting lifestyle and made significant dietary changes, including following a strict anti-inflammatory diet. My joint inflammation was so severe that I could only do Pilates and water aerobics without considerable pain. I surrounded my journey in continual prayer and had some accountability partners. Slowly but surely, my health began to improve.

Over two years later, I have lost eighty pounds and significantly improved my mobility. I am far more active and have the energy to serve God enthusiastically, so praise God!

The Importance of Self-Care

Through my own journey, I learned that self-care is not selfish or self-indulgent—it is necessary. We cannot effectively serve others or fulfill our God-given purposes if we neglect our health. We must contribute to God's plan for our lives by being at our very best and demonstrating the fruit of self-control. Let's work to preserve our energy levels to reap the harvest—the time is short!

These times of quiet reflection and being alone are a great time to process things with God and assess where He may be guiding you. Sometimes, we just get too busy to listen to where He is leading. I've known people who lost a loved one, went through a divorce, or had their children move out, and they never took the time to process their grief/life change with God. Staying busy is really just a form of avoiding pain. God wants us to sit in pain with Him. After all, there is a book of the bible titled Lamentations!

> Lamentations 3:25-26 "The Lord is good to those whose hope is in him, to the one who seeks him; it is good to wait quietly for the salvation of the Lord."

7. *Intellectual Pursuits.* If you have an interest in apologetics, prophecy, or some other topic, take some time to research it. Could you write a journal about what you are learning and share the information with others? Write a blog about it, send it to Crazy Praise Club, and we may feature it on our website. However, it's essential to remember that whatever you are studying must align with Scripture, so always test the information you're learning against God's Word.

The Crazy Praise Club website, www.crazypraiseclub.com, has several online master classes and resources for you to pursue. We have cultivated relationships with several local experts in various aspects of ministry, and they teach our master classes. Not surprisingly, my class is on the Transformative Power of Praise!

Check back often as we are continually adding new resources and experts for you to explore.

Interacting with Others

As we engage in these activities, we can come to recognize the unique spiritual gifts God has bestowed upon us. These gifts are not merely for personal edification but are tools for praising God and serving others. Reflect on your spiritual gifts—teaching, hospitality, encouragement, creativity, or other gifts—and consider how you can use these gifts in interactive praise activities. For instance, if you have the gift of hospitality, invite friends over for a meal and share testimonies of God's goodness, creating an atmosphere of praise.

As we embrace our spiritual gifts in worship with others, we align our hearts with God's purpose, transforming our praise into a collective expression of love and service. This interaction deepens our connection with one another and God, creating a joyful community of hearts transformed through praise.

In this chapter, we have explored the journey of praise through reflecting inward, knowing Jesus upward, and expanding outward. May we all embrace the call to engage in interactive praise activities, allowing our hearts to overflow with joy and gratitude as we serve the One who deserves all our praise. In the next chapter, we will look more deeply into expanding outward—that is, what praise looks like in community.

WISDOM MEETS GROWTH: THE BENEFITS OF BRAIN DEVELOPMENT

What are the benefits of learning a new skill later in life? As you embrace new praise practices keep in mind the practical bene- fits of learning a new skill later in life. The challenges presented by learning enrich your personal and professional life in many ways. Here are some key advantages:

COGNITIVE STIMULATION: Engaging in new activities stimulates the brain, promoting neuroplasticity and enhancing memory and overall cognitive function. This mental challenge keeps the mind sharp, prevents cognitive decline and can even combat aging.

INCREASED CONFIDENCE: Mastering a new skill can boost self-esteem and confidence. When we master a challenge, we reinforce a sense of achievement and capability, which spills over into other areas of life.

SOCIAL CONNECTIONS: New activitities can mean joining classes or groups, which provides opportunities to meet new people and build social networks. These connections can lead to lasting friendships while building a sense of community.

ENHANCED CREATIVITY: Exploring new skills fosters creativity, encouraging thinking outside the box and approaching problems from different angles. This creative energy can cause you to seek innovative ideas in many areas of life.

IMPROVED ADAPTABILITY: Learning something new helps develop adaptability and resilience. Tackling a challenge prepares you to embrace change and navigate life's challenges more effectively.

PHYSICAL BENEFITS: If the new skill is physical (like dancing, gardening, or sports), it can improve physical health, increase mobility, and enhance overall well-being, contributing to a more active lifestyle and general wellness.

FULFILLMENT AND PURPOSE: It's exciting to reignite passions or help us discover new interests, in fact leading to greater fulfillment and a sense of purpose. This can enhance overall life satisfaction.

LIFELONG LEARNING MINDSET: Committing to learning throughout life fosters a growth mindset, encouraging curiosity and a love for learning that is inspirational.Career Opportunities: Acquiring new skills can enhance employability and open doors to new career paths or advancements, further contributing to your expertise on the subject.

STRESS RELIEF: Becoming focused on a new skill can be a productive distraction from daily stresses, providing an outlet for relaxation and enjoyment.

Learning a new skill later in life can significantly enhance cognitive function, social connections, personal fulfillment, and overall quality of life. So jump start your creative praise, and remember it's never too late to embark on a new journey of discovery and growth!

Scripture References: Psalm 150; Hebrews 10:24–25

Prov 1:5 "Let the wise listen and add to their learning, and the the discerning get guidance."

THE POWER OF COMMUNITY

The Transformative Power of Praise
in Building Community through Creative Experiences

In the previous chapter, we explored the transformative power of innovative and creative worship, which ignites our intimacy with God and Jesus. Coming together with others in heartfelt praise and earnest prayer deepens our connection with the Lord and fortifies our bonds with one another. The shared worship experience becomes a tapestry of voices and hearts as we gather, weaving us closer together in our shared faith and community.

Creative experiences can transform individuals and communities through music, art, drama, or any other form of expression. Engaging in these experiences can deepen our understanding of God and His love for us and strengthen our bonds. This chapter will delve into the transformative power of praise through creative experiences and how it can build a strong and united community.

We will revisit some of the activity ideas from the last chapter, but our focus here is on building community through shared creative experiences. So, we're taking a slightly different approach to praise here but one that is equally rewarding. Let's dive in!

Unity through Music

Music is a powerful expression that speaks to the soul and can move us profoundly. Historically, music has been used in religious settings to praise and worship God. The book of Psalms in the Bible is a collection of songs and poems used to praise God. Psalm 150:4–5 says, "Praise Him with tambourine and dance; praise Him with strings and pipe! Praise Him with sounding cymbals; praise Him with loud clashing cymbals!" (ESV).

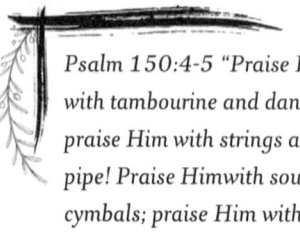

Psalm 150:4-5 "Praise Him with tambourine and dance; praise Him with strings and pipe! Praise Himwith sounding cymbals; praise Him with loud clashing cymbals."

I imagine these praise incidents in Psalms as impromptu jam sessions where everyone grabs an instrument and breaks out into songs to the Lord! These could be intimate gatherings or the entire king's court. In either case, these worship sessions would catalyze incredible growth as a community—the best night of praise you could imagine.

When we come together in a community to praise God, we lift our voices in worship and create a beautiful harmony that unites us. Whether singing hymns, Contemporary Christian songs, or our own compositions, music making in a group setting can be a transformative experience. Shut your eyes and soak in the presence of the Lord as you worship Him, and feel unity of spirit with those around you.

Music opens up a space for vulnerability and authenticity within a community. When we sing together, we are not just singing for ourselves but for one another and God. We share our hearts and voices and can connect deeper in that vulnerability. This can foster a sense of belonging and togetherness within the community.

Furthermore, studies have shown that singing together in a group can release endorphins and oxytocin, the "feel-good" hormones, increasing feelings of trust and bonding among individuals. As we sing and worship, we build our relationship with God and a stronger and more connected community.

When wholly invested in praise and worship, we are indeed free. Praise music is a weapon against the powers of darkness. It is a vehicle to usher in the presence of God. Certain songs may move us to tears or cause us to jump for joy or drop to our knees in humility. Music has that power.

My friend and I enjoy singing Handel's "Messiah" at Christmas each year. We have our scores, practice with YouTube at home, then go to a sing-along. I have been singing "Messiah" since high school, and now I'm (ahem) several decades beyond that. I know the entire score by heart.

Yet, there is something powerful about singing this music alongside others who revere the Lord. The music transports me to where I have transcended earth, but I'm not quite in heaven. There is camaraderie, with other believers joining with me and me with them to create a powerful manifestation of voices raised to honor our heavenly Father. It brings a high that lasts several days! I simply cannot get through "The Hallelujah Chorus" without shedding a tear!

Unity through Art

Art is another form of creative expression that has the power to transform and build community. In Exodus 35:30–35, we read about how God equipped specific individuals with artistic skills to create sacred objects for worship in the tabernacle. This shows us that God values the use of art in worship and that it can be a powerful tool for connecting with Him and with one another.

Consider how this cadre of artisans with different skills came together to honor God with their collective skills. Can you imagine the joy and unity of reporting to work each day when building the tabernacle was your project? In this single passage, we see all these skills and talents being used for the

Exodus 25:24 - 36:1
"Then Moses said to the Isrealites, 'See, the LORD has chosen Bezalel son of Uri, the son of Hur, of the tribe of Judah, and he has filled him with the Spirit of God, with skill, ability and knowledge in all kinds of crafts - to make artistic designs for work in gold, silver and bronze, to cut and set stones, to work in wood and to engage in all kinds of artistic craftsmanship. And he has given both im and Oholiab sone of Ahisimach, of the tribe of Dan, the ability to teach others. He has filled them with skill to do all kinds of work as crafts-men, designers, embroiderers in blue, purple and scarlet yarn and fine linen, and weavers - all of them master craftsmen and designers. So Behalele, Oholiab and every skilled person to whom the Lord has given skill and ability know how to carry out the work of constructing the sanctuary are do do the work just as the Lord commanded."

Lord; metal workers, stone cutters, gem stone craftsmen, woodworking, embroiderers, weavers, and working with cloth. But the best part of this passage is Moses telling us that these craftsmen were filled with the Spirit of God in creating their masterpieces for His glory. So when any kind of artistic skills are dedicated to God, He will view them as an act of praise!

Creating art together can be a unifying experience, as it allows individuals to come together and collaborate on a common goal. When we engage in art making as a community, we can see each other's unique perspectives and talents and appreciate the diversity within our communities. This can break down barriers and bring us closer together as we work toward a shared vision.

Moreover, art can be a form of storytelling and help us express our thoughts and emotions visually. When we create art in response to our faith and worship, we praise God and share our personal experiences and testimonies. This can deepen our understanding of one another and create a sense of empathy and compassion within the community.

Unity through Drama

Drama is another creative avenue for praising and worshiping God in a community setting. The Bible contains dramatic stories and parables that Jesus used to teach His disciples and followers. Matthew 13:34 says, "Jesus spoke all these things to the crowd in parables; He did not say anything to them without using a parable."

When we engage in dramatic experiences together, such as skits, plays, or interactive storytelling, we can bring to life the stories and teachings of the Bible in new and impactful ways. This helps us better understand and remember God's Word and creates a sense of unity and fellowship within the community.

Drama can also be a powerful tool for reflection and self-discovery. When we act out biblical stories or characters, we put ourselves in their shoes and can better understand their struggles and triumphs. This can help us to relate to one another and build empathy and compassion within the community.

In the intimate setting of my small group, our dedicated facilitator spent the entire last year guiding us through an enriching study of the women in the Bible. In each session, a different group member was chosen to bring the story of her assigned biblical woman to life, and she was encouraged to express her tale in any creative manner in which she felt inspired. Some women donned elaborate costumes, embodying their characters as they recited monologues or read Scripture passages passionately. Others chose a more straightforward approach, engaging us with talks about their woman's characteristics, her significant role in the Scriptures, and the lessons she imparted. One particularly imaginative retired teacher captivated us with a lively trivia game and quiz, making the learning experience interactive and fun.

When my turn came, I presented a skit, performed alongside two other enthusiastic ladies, in which we dramatized our stories with flair. The varied ways the women in our group honored these biblical women mirrored the diversity of the participants and their subjects. Through this shared journey, we each experienced profound growth and connection. And you can bet we will remember those stories!

Arts as Therapy and Healing

The arts have the power to heal and restore individuals and communities. They allow us to express ourselves in ways that words cannot and help us make sense of our thoughts and emotions. As Christians, we believe God is the ultimate healer, and the arts can help us connect with His healing power.

At a widow's retreat, I witnessed how journal making gave participants a way to express their grief—many for the first time. The event occurred right after the COVID pandemic, and many of these women were young and left to shoulder the burden of single-handedly raising their young children as well as having lost their life partner. Where words failed them, the journal-making process of documenting their journey finally allowed the healing power to open up a way forward and bring praise back to their lives. I observed the tears running down their faces as the Lord healed them through this artistic journey. Sharing this experience gave widows a sense of unity and community with others who loved the Lord but were also struggling.

Moreover, there is growing evidence supporting the use of art therapy in modern psychological counseling. Art therapy involves using different forms of artistic expression to help individuals work through emotional or psychological issues. It reduces stress and anxiety, improves self-esteem, and promotes overall well-being. Art is shown to be able to break down emotional walls that mere words cannot.

As Christians, we know that God is the ultimate healer. Through art therapy, we can connect with His healing power and allow Him to restore our minds and hearts.

Expressing Our Pain through Art

Putting our feelings into words can be challenging in times of suffering or pain. However, the arts provide an outlet for us to express these emotions tangibly. This is especially true for those who struggle with mental health issues or trauma.

Through creating art, individuals can externalize their internal struggles and process their pain safely and non-threateningly. This helps them cope with their challenges and allows them to experience God's healing touch through the creative process. Art can be lifesaving for those who may not have well-developed traditional verbal or written-communication skills.

In addition, sharing our art with others who may be going through similar struggles creates a sense of empathy and understanding within the community. We are reminded that we are not alone in our pain but are part of a larger community that supports and cares for one another.

The Transformative Power of Praise in Action

Now that we have explored how creative experiences can be used to praise and worship God, let's examine some real-life examples of how they have transformed and built communities.

One example is the Voices of Unity choir in South Africa. This choir comprises individuals from diverse backgrounds and cultures who come together to sing praises to God. Through their music, they break down racial and cultural barriers and create a space of unity and love. Their music's power has transformed their lives and the lives of those who have listened to them.

Another example is the 1,000 Hallelujahs project in Brazil, where individuals from different churches and backgrounds composed and recorded a song of praise to God. This project aimed to unite people from differing denominations and backgrounds, bringing together a diverse community of believers and creating a sense of solidarity and love.

The global impact of the series *The Chosen* demonstrates how powerful storytelling can be. I recently read an account from Jonathan Roumie, the

EXPRESSING OUR PAIN THROUGH ART

What painful event or season of your life can you express to God through art? Use this space to sketch, draw or articulate an expression of a a painful time to God. Then, hand it over to Him to take you on a journey of healing and restoration.

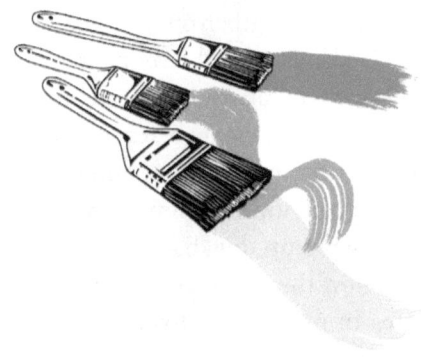

actor portraying Jesus in the series. He talks about how, during one particular scene, he began weeping because he felt so unworthy to be speaking the words of Jesus. He had to step aside with the director to understand and appreciate the impact his portrayal was having, and then he was able to proceed with humility.

These examples show us the transformative power of praise and the power of building community through creative experiences. When we come together as a community to engage in these experiences, we strengthen our relationship with God and strengthen our relationships with one another. We can break down barriers, create a sense of belonging and togetherness, and make a strong and united community.

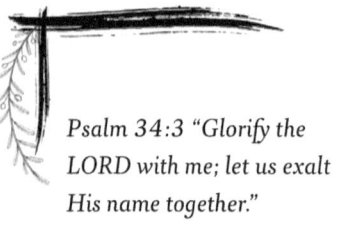

Psalm 34:3 "Glorify the LORD with me; let us exalt His name together."

To wrap up this discussion, consider how the use of creative experiences in praising and worshipping God has the potential to transform and build your community. Whether through music, art, drama, or any other form of expression, these experiences deepen our relationship with God and bring us closer to one another. As we continue using our gifts and talents to praise and glorify God, let us remember the transformative power of creative praise in building a strong and united community. As it says in Psalm 34:3, "Glorify the LORD with me; let us exalt His name together." Together, let us praise and glorify God and, in the process, build a community that reflects His love and unity.

TIME FOR CRAZY PRAISE

1. **EXPLORE COMMUNAL PRAISE**. Journal Prompt - Go to YouTube or another streaming platform, and search for videos that, to you, represent the power of communal worship. In the space below, write about how the experience might have impacted you if you were a part of it.

2. **MY CREATIVE TRIBE.** Draw or write descriptions of some of the people or communities in your life where you experience the collective power of creative praise. Next to each, answer the connection: What can I do to deepen my connection here? You may want to jot down specific actions and dates you will take to grow.

3. **SERVING OTHERS.** In previous chapters, we've explored your unique giftings and passions. In the space below, journal about how you can use these to contribute to the growth of your Christian community. If you have any creative leanings or talents, how can you use those to grow your community?

PERSONAL PRACTICES
FOR SPIRITUAL INTIMACY

Transformative Praise

We have established that praise is a powerful tool in our spiritual journey. It can transform our hearts, minds, and souls and draw us closer to God. As believers, it is essential to cultivate a habit of praise in our daily lives, not just in our church services or Sunday worship.

We have discussed the powerful ways collective praise can build community. Though we have touched on the concept of individual praise already, in this chapter, we will delve more deeply into the personal practice of transformative praise and how it can deepen our intimacy with God.

I am convinced that the Lord finds joy in our communal worship and acts of praise. Together, we aim to capture every thought for Christ! Yet, in those serene, personal moments, we can genuinely connect with the gentle, whispering presence of the Holy Spirit. In these instances, the world falls away, and a sacred silence envelopes us, allowing us to listen with our hearts attuned to the divine guidance that speaks softly within us. Sometimes, we can have these highly personal experiences even when in the company of others.

For reasons I have yet to understand, I get highly emotional at times during worship. I suppose it's the Spirit of God moving in me. This used to really embarrass me to the point of apologizing, yet it seemed beyond my control. I have since learned to take that time to spend one-on-one with God and appreciate the experience and be grateful for it, not embarrassed by it. These experiences remind us of the nearness of the Lord, and they are opportunities for us to express our deep gratitude and praise to Him.

Creative Expressions of Our Love for the Lord

One of the beautiful things about praise is that it can be expressed in countless ways. It is not just limited to singing songs or reciting prayers but can also be demonstrated through our actions and attitudes. Here are some creative expressions of our love for the Lord through praise that we can pursue in our personal practice of praise:

1. Dancing before the Lord. The Bible contains examples of people dancing before the Lord in praise and adoration. King David danced with all his might when the ark of the covenant was brought into Jerusalem (2 Samuel 6:14). Dancing is a physical expression of our joy and love for God. It is a way to relinquish our inhibitions and surrender ourselves entirely to Him.

2. Creating Art for God. God is the ultimate Creator, and we are made in His image. Therefore, using our creative gifts to praise and worship Him is only fitting. This can be through painting, drawing, sculpting, or any other form of art that we pursue in solitude. Creating something for God is an act not just of praise but also of surrender and obedience.

I enjoy doodling with colored markers on sketch pads. I choose a word (*grace, dream, surrender*) or image (heart, flower, cross, sheep) and select colors and pictures that appeal to me. I have done some lovely drawings, just doodling while meditating on Scripture or listening to praise music. Sometimes, I might add some stickers, stamps, scrapbook 3D images, or scraps of decorative paper or fabrics. Often, I have gifted these to people God puts on my heart, not thinking they are much of anything, only to find that the recipients are really moved by the pieces. It's not necessarily because they're especially good—it's because they come from the heart.

3. Writing Songs or Poems. Like King David, we can pour out our hearts to God through songs and poems. They don't have to be professionally produced or published, but a simple melody or a heartfelt poem can be a sweet offering to the Lord. These expressions of praise can also serve as personal reminders of God's goodness and faithfulness in our lives. I imagine Jesus lights up when we sing an original song to Him, no matter how humble! I still have a secret dream of one day writing a Christian musical—you heard me!

4. Serving Others in His Name. Jesus said, "Truly I tell you, whatever you did for one of the least of these brothers and sisters of Mine, you did for Me" (Matthew 25:40). When we serve others, we also serve God. This can be a powerful form of praise as it demonstrates our love for the Lord by showing love to others. I previously thought of myself as somewhat selfish, and I asked the Lord many years ago to humble me through serving others to break that in me. Now, I just love serving others, and that's what truly brings me joy.

5. Journaling or Writing. We often struggle to express our deepest thoughts and feelings. However, journaling or writing can be a powerful way to communicate with God. It allows us to pour out our hearts and minds, laying everything before Him intimately and personally.

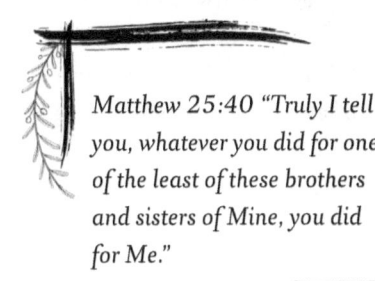

Matthew 25:40 "Truly I tell you, whatever you did for one of the least of these brothers and sisters of Mine, you did for Me."

Writing helps us process our thoughts and emotions. Often, when we write down our thoughts and feelings, we come to understand them better. This is especially true of our relationship with God. As we put pen to paper, we can pause and reflect on what we feel and think about God. This can lead us to a deeper understanding and intimacy with Him.

Many times, I open a blank page in my journal feeling perfectly neutral about myself or something happening in my life. But then, as I start writing without stopping except for drink breaks from my water bottle, by the time I look up at the clock, hours have passed! I thank the Lord over and over for His faithfulness, in tears at how I can see His hand on me as reflected through each day's happenings.

Creating a Personal Sanctuary or Prayer Space

In the movie *War Room*, the main character, Elizabeth, has a designated prayer room where she spends time with God. This room serves as her sanctuary where she can pour out her heart to God and listen to His voice.

Like Elizabeth, we need a dedicated space for prayer and intimate time with God. Here are some ideas for creating a personal sanctuary:

1. Find a Quiet and Comfortable Space. It could be a room in your house, a corner of your bedroom, or even a spot in your backyard. The key is to choose a place where you can have some privacy and focus on God without distractions.

MY PERSONAL SANCTUARY WITH THE LORD

What kind of space is the ideal sanctuary for you to connect with God? In the space below, draw or describe some of the items you want to include.

Where will your space be located?

What personal items do you want to include in your sanctuary?

2. Personalize It. Make the space your own by adding elements that bring you closer to God. These could be a cross, a painting of Jesus, your favorite Bible verses, scented candles, or anything else that helps create a peaceful and inviting atmosphere.

I recently heard a teaching in which the presenter challenged us to find an image of Jesus that we relate to and post it somewhere we can see it. I love this idea, and I'm searching for my unique piece of art! Be cognizant that this art, whether it be an image of Jesus, a cross, prayer beads or something else, is merely a representation of our Lord, and not something that we should worship in and of itself.

The same can be said of beautiful, decorative crosses. Crosses can be a lovely representation of our Lord's sacrifice for us, but in and of themselves the cross holds no magical power. You can display and enjoy crosses, but be careful to only worship the one who hung on the cross for you, and not the cross itself.

3. Use It Consistently. Make using your sanctuary a habit. Set aside a specific time to pray and worship in this space each day. Initially, it may take some discipline, but it will become a natural and cherished part of your day. It will also become a special place where you can steal away to spend time alone with God, and we all need that from time to time.

4. Keep It Clutter-Free. A cluttered space can distract and hinder your connection with God. Keep your sanctuary clean and organized to focus on Him entirely. You may wish to keep a prayer journal, prayer wall, or prayer jar where you keep requests to pray. Remember to note when your prayers are answered and thank Him!

Practical Ways to Grow Intimacy with God

Praise is not just a one-time event but a continual practice that helps us grow in our intimacy with God. As we draw closer to Him through praise, we will experience His love, grace, and presence in a deeper and more meaningful way. Here are some practical ways to cultivate intimacy with God through transformative praise:

1. Read and Meditate on His Word. The Bible is God's love letter, filled with promises, wisdom, and instructions for our lives. Meditating on God's Word fills our minds and hearts with His truth and draws us closer to Him.

If you struggle to read and grasp the meaning of God's Word, remember that there are alternative methods to immerse yourself in Scripture. I enjoy playing my audio Bible during car time, letting the soothing narration fill the car as I navigate through traffic. Additionally, I often turn to the "Bible Recap" on YouTube. In this series, host Tara-Leigh Cobble breaks down each chapter of the Bible with clarity and simplicity, offering insights that make the lessons more accessible and easier to digest. There are plenty of resources online and in books to help you understand difficult passages of the Bible.

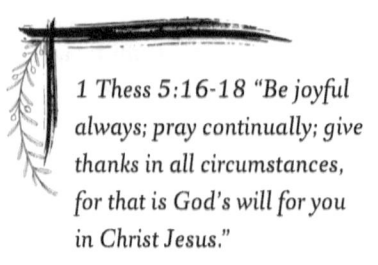

1 Thess 5:16-18 "Be joyful always; pray continually; give thanks in all circumstances, for that is God's will for you in Christ Jesus."

When people tell me they struggle reading scripture, I am quick to recommend audio or video resources. You may recall from an earlier chapter that each of these methods of digesting scripture lights up a different part of the brain, so one is likely to create more of a response than the others. I recently recommended *Bible Recap* to a friend with dyslexia who struggles with reading. He loves it, finally scripture is more accessible to him!

2. *Pray without Ceasing.* The Bible tells us to "pray without ceasing" (1 Thessalonians 5:17 ESV). This doesn't mean we have to be on our knees all day—instead, we can have an ongoing conversation with God throughout the day. This constant communication builds a deeper intimacy and trust in our relationship with Him.

3. *Practice Gratitude.* One of the most potent ways to praise God is through gratitude. When we focus on His goodness and faithfulness, we are reminded of His love for us, and our hearts are filled with thankfulness. Make it a daily practice to write down things you are grateful for and thank God for them.

When I was finally able to buy a home a few years ago, I was so grateful that I made it a practice that every time I enter my home, I say a quick prayer of gratitude and invite the Holy Spirit to inhabit this dwelling place to instruct and protect me. I've been in my home over 4 years now, and this has become firmly ingrained in my routine now. People say they can feel the anointing in my home – I can't think of a better compliment.

4. *Sing and Listen to Worship Music.* Music has a way of stirring our souls and uniquely connecting us with God. Spend time singing and listening to

worship songs, allowing godly lyrics to penetrate your heart and draw you closer to Him.

5. *Share Your Testimony.* As believers, we have all experienced God's goodness and faithfulness. Sharing our testimonies is a powerful way to praise God and encourage others in their faith journeys. Prepare a handful of "God stories" that are easy to share and can incite meaningful conversations.

In conclusion, transformative praise is not just about singing or reciting rote prayers. It is a lifestyle of creatively expressing our love for God, creating a personal sanctuary for time with Him, and actively seeking ways to grow in our intimacy with Him. May we all cultivate a habit of transformative praise and experience a deeper and more intimate relationship with our heavenly Father.

TIME FOR CRAZY PRAISE

PERSONAL TESTIMONY WORKSHEET

How I came to know Jesus -

What my faith journey has been like for me -

Times when I felt God protecting me -

My greatest seasons of growth occurred when

What Christ means to me -

Now that you've thought through the highlights of your personal testimony, where can you boldly share it with others as a demonstration of what Christ has done for you? Perhaps in a church group, host a testimonial dinner or seek out others with similar challenges as you've faced to encourage them.

EMBRACING THE UNEXPECTED

Life is full of surprises—some good, some bad. We plan and prepare for the expected, but the unexpected tests our adaptability and resilience. Unforeseen events give us unique opportunities to praise, challenging us to adapt and find the beauty and value in the unexpected.

Remember this: nothing that happens to you surprises God. He loves you, is with you, and is waiting for you to invite Him into every situation in your life.

Praise is a powerful tool that can lift spirits, boost confidence, and strengthen relationships. Most importantly, it is how we build intimacy with God. It is easy to praise when things are going well, but praising in unexpected moments—even moments of profound pain or loss—takes a unique mindset. These moments catch us off guard, challenge our perceptions, and ultimately push us to grow and evolve.

Someone recently remarked, "There is always purpose in pain." This resonated deeply with me, as it is indeed true. Amid our trials, God gently teaches us about our natures and, even more significantly, unveils the depths of His character to us. These revelations become most profound during the challenging times when we manage to lift our voices in praise despite our suffering.

In this chapter, we will explore the power of embracing unexpected opportunities to praise and how it can enhance our lives and the lives of those around us. We will delve into examples of unforeseen opportunities for praise and the profound impact they can have. So, let's dive in and discover the beauty of praising the unexpected.

The Beauty in the Unexpected

Life is unpredictable, and that's what makes it so beautiful. We can plan and prepare, but ultimately, we have no control over the future. Unexpected opportunities for praise can arise in moments of unpredictability.

Getting caught up in life's routine and taking things for granted is easy. But what about the moments that take us outside of our routine? These moments catch us by surprise and remind us of the beauty of life. These are when we have opportunities to learn more about God and what He values.

Unexpected opportunities for praise teach us about ourselves and reveal God's character uniquely and profoundly. What are some things God can reveal about Himself when we worship and praise Him in unexpected moments?

1. His Sovereignty. The unexpected often reminds us of our lack of control over our lives. However, it also powerfully reminds us of God's sovereignty and control over everything. When we face unexpected challenges or blessings, we are reminded that God is ultimately in control and can work all things for our good.

2. His Provision. In moments of uncertainty or loss, God often provides unexpected blessings and support we could not have planned for. These moments remind us that God is our provider and will care for our needs even when we least expect it. Sometimes, when we lose a loved one, for example, we are surprised at how many people are there to support and pray for us. We see God's provision in our darkest hour.

3. His Faithfulness. When life throws curveballs at us, it can be easy to doubt God's faithfulness. But in these moments, when we choose to praise Him despite our circumstances, we see His unwavering commitment to us. He remains faithful even when things don't go as planned. As a single person who has navigated job loss, broken relationships, financial struggles, and health issues, I have had to master the art of praising in all my circumstances. Sometimes, it has just been God and me together working through things.

4. His Grace. Sometimes, the unexpected reveals painful truths about ourselves or others. We may feel overwhelmed with guilt or anger in these moments, but God offers us grace and forgiveness if we humble ourselves before Him. We can experience the full extent of God's grace through unexpected opportunities for praise. His grace is why we should not be self-conscious about our abilities or skills. He is delighted that His child is offering Him such a sweet gift.

5. His Miracles. God often works miracles in the most unexpected ways and times. These moments remind us of His power and ability to do the impossible in our lives and the world around us.

6. *His Love*. It can be easy to question whether God truly loves us in seasons of suffering or loss. But through praising Him in unexpected situations, we learn more deeply that His love is unconditional and unwavering.

7. *His Purpose*. The beauty in the unexpected is often found in the purpose that it reveals. It may be that God wants to draw you closer to Himself. Or, He could be guiding you to a new passion project or service area. Sometimes, it can be about the people you meet along the journey. Keep your mind and heart open to all God is doing.

The Courage to Praise the Unexpected

Embracing unexpected opportunities to praise requires courage to step out of our comfort zones and be vulnerable. Praising the unpredictable is not always easy, especially when we are faced with real tragedy.

A very close friend of mine lost her brother unexpectedly this past summer. It was a horrible circumstance. He was simply eating his dinner at a tavern, and someone shot him from behind as he whirled around, sensing danger. My friend was extremely close to her brother—they spoke every day. She has been battling profound grief, and there is a lengthy court battle that continually reminds her of how her brother died.

But since his passing, beautiful things have emerged like blossoms in a barren field. The outpouring of love at his funeral revealed his profound depth of character and a tapestry of life experiences my friend never imagined. Now, she stands at a crossroads—one path is shaded by the heavy cloak of grief that threatens to stifle her voice. The other path is bathed in the light of courage, urging her to honor the memory of her loved one by embracing the positive impact he had on so many lives. With a heart full of resolve, she has chosen the path of praise, lifting her voice in gratitude to God for her brother's life, for the countless cherished years they shared, and most importantly, for the promise that she will see him again one day.

In the wake of this tragedy, she has allowed God to work through her in new and profound ways. Her leadership has blossomed, her walk has strengthened, and her powerful testimony is changing lives!

When we dare to give God praise in the unexpected, it not only positively impacts us but also allows us to learn and grow. We open ourselves up to new perspectives and ideas, and in turn, we become more open-minded and adaptable individuals.

Examples of Unexpected Opportunities for Praise

Now that we understand the beauty and courage of embracing unexpected opportunities to praise, let's examine some examples—just a few of the countless moments that can arise in our lives that have the potential for profound impact.

1. Praise through Empathy and Compassion. We live in a fast-paced world, constantly rushing from one task to another. Amidst our bustling lives, our praise to God can be manifested in how we treat others. Even when we don't feel kind, we can defer to the Holy Spirit and show kindness anyway, and that becomes our witness. We can take the opportunity daily to express our praise to God through our empathy and compassion for others.

Our unexpected acts of kindness, like the Good Samaritan in the Bible, who cared for a needy stranger, are a form of praise. They reflect Christ's teachings to love and serve others selflessly. We can also acknowledge and praise God in moments when we see others spread the spirit of Christ's love and kindness through their acts of compassion.

2. Praise in Resilience. Life is full of challenges and setbacks, and it is in these moments that your resilience is truly tested. When you face unexpected hurdles, getting discouraged and giving up are easy. But if you rise and push through the difficulties, your resilience becomes an expression of praise. You are demonstrating God's presence in your life in all circumstances.

Recall a time when you faced numerous setbacks but persevered and eventually succeeded. Instead of just celebrating the result, take a moment to praise God for your resilience throughout the entire process. Praising in these moments can make all the difference and encourage others to keep pushing through future challenges.

3. Praise through Creativity and Innovation. We often associate creativity and innovation with artists, designers, and entrepreneurs. But the truth is that creativity and innovation are rooted in our heavenly Father and can be found in all aspects of life. We serve a creative God—one need only look around at nature to see it! We can face the unexpected with creative and innovative solutions and acknowledge the source of that creativity. This can surprise us and inspire others to tap into their hidden resources.

As mentioned earlier, God is the ultimate source of creativity. When we seek His inspiration through prayer and reading His Word, our minds become open to new ideas and solutions. We may find inspiration in unexpected places or everyday situations.

For example, while tending sheep in Midian, Moses did not expect God's call to lead His people out of Egypt (Exodus 3). But he was receptive when God spoke through a burning bush, and he obediently followed God's plan. Similarly, we must be open to God's leading and inspiration in our own lives.

4. *Praise in Growth and Learning.* We often think of praise as a response to success and achievement, but it is equally important to praise during the process of growth and learning. When we embrace unexpected opportunities to praise when God is stretching us, we honor Him with our teachability and willingness to grow. We also encourage others to continue evolving and fully surrendering to the Lord.

In my career, I have had many opportunities to receive training and learn new skills. At times, the skills (and timetables!) I am required to master are quite challenging. I can remember a tough season when I started a new job, and less than a month later, I had to do a new project launch. The prospect was daunting. On my first day on the job, following a long season of unemployment, I knew I had to succeed in this challenge. So, I anointed my desk and laptop with oil, prayed in surrender, and called on the Lord for guidance. That project was a smashing success, and I reveled in telling everyone I did it with God's help.

The Impact of Embracing Unexpected Opportunities to Praise

The transformative power of praising when faced with the unexpected is genuinely remarkable. Praise builds a strong connection with your Father and has a ripple effect on those around you. In times of suffering, your praise directs your focus toward the One who walks with you through the dark valley. You may want to re-read this book's Foreward by my dear friend, author Amanda Hayhurst, who shares an example of how praise impacted her life when her young son was diagnosed with leukemia.

When we face the unexpected with praise, we create a climate of expectation, appreciation, and positivity, even when we face struggles. We inspire others to see the beauty in the ashes and to have the courage to praise through their challenges. We also open ourselves to new perspectives and insights, allowing us to grow and evolve. Above all else, we allow Christ to shine through us in our attitude and assurance when we see Him at work!

I have a great example of this from my own life. I unexpectedly lost my job last fall, right before the holiday season. Instead of panicking, I immediately seized the opportunity to do some writing and build some workshops. The result is this book, the Crazy Praise Club website, a series of live workshops, and the design of online courses.

The next time you encounter an unexpected moment, don't miss the opportunity to praise. Instead of focusing on understanding God (*why* something happened), focus on trusting God (*how* can I grow through this?). You never know the profound impact it can have—not just on your faith journey but as an example to others. Trust God with your circumstances, it's not a surprise to Him. Embrace the unexpected and watch the beauty and magic unfold.

TIME FOR CRAZY PRAISE

UNEXPECTED PRAISE OPPORTUNITY
Think back over your life, and make a mental note of 3-4 times when you encountered an unexpected loss or profound grief. Perhaps you struggled with trying to understand why it happened. Now, pray for God to reveal to you the ways you grew in these seasons, and what God show you about himself.

Event description -

How God grew me through this -

OVERCOMING FEAR
TO EXPERIENCE VICTORY

The Power of Praise

Fear. It is an emotion that we have all experienced at some point in our lives. Whether it is fear of the unknown, fear of failure, or fear of rejection, it can paralyze us and prevent us from living the abundant life that God has promised us.

But what if I told you that there is a powerful weapon we can use to overcome fear? Generations before us have used this weapon, and it has proven adequate time and time again. That weapon is spiritual praise. Praise is such a powerful weapon for overcoming fear that it deserves special attention in its own chapter.

We have three weapons to experience spiritual victory at any time: Scripture, prayer, and praise. Whenever we engage any of these things, we are wholly focused on God, and the Holy Spirit moves within us. When I am afraid and don't know what to do, one of my favorite things is to loudly sing a praise song. Embrace your weapons wholeheartedly, without reservation. God put them there for our use, so let's use them!

Praise is not just singing songs or reciting prayers. This spiritual practice involves acknowledging and exalting God's greatness and goodness. It is an act of surrender and trust, coming from the belief that God is in control and has the power to overcome any fear or obstacle in our lives. When we unleash a practice of spiritual praise in our lives, we tap into a supernatural source of strength and peace that empowers us to overcome fear.

In the book of Psalms, we see the psalmist repeatedly using praise to overcome fear. In Psalm 34, David writes, "I will bless the LORD at all times; His praise shall continually be in my mouth. My soul makes its boast in the LORD;

Write, draw or express the

victory weapon

God has given you
to praise Him with

(Scripture, Prayer, Praise)

Your Spiritual Weapons

When Jesus left this earth, he promised to send an advocate to help us and be with us forever, namely the Holy Spirit. He also says in John 14:16-17 that "the wor"d cannot accept him, because it neither sees him nor knows him. But YOU know him, for he will be with you! Here are 3 ways we can access the power of Holy Spirit.

Scripture

For the word of the God is alive and active. Sharper than any double-edged sward, it penetrates even to dividing soul and spirit, joints and marrow; it judges the thoughts and attitudes of the heart. -Hebrews 4:12

Prayer

Call to me and I will answer you and tell you great and unsearchable things you do not know - Jeremiah 33:3

Praise

May the praise of God be in their mouths and a double-edged sword in their hands. - Pslam 149:6

let the humble hear and be glad. Oh, magnify the LORD with me, and let us exalt His name together!" (Psalm 34:1–3 ESV).

Here, David declares that he will continually praise God no matter his circumstances. He acknowledges that God is more significant than any fear or problem and invites others to glorify God. This is a powerful example of how we can overcome fear through the practice of spiritual praise.

Psalm 56:3-4 "When I am afraid, I put my trust in You. In God, whose Word I praise, in God I trust; I shall not be afraid. What can flesh do to me?"

In addition to the examples in Psalms, we see the power of praise in the story of Jehoshaphat in 2 Chronicles 20. When faced with an overwhelming army, Jehoshaphat and the people of Judah turned to God and praised Him. They declared, "Give thanks to the LORD, for His steadfast love endures forever" (2 Chronicles 20:21 ESV). As they praised, the Lord fought for them, and they experienced a miraculous victory over their enemies. This story shows us that when we praise God, He goes before us and fights our battles.

But, you may wonder, how can we praise God when we are consumed by fear? The answer is that God has given us the power to praise Him even when we are scared. In Philippians 4:13, Paul writes, "I can do all things through Him who strengthens me" (ESV). Here, Paul reminds us that it is through God's strength that we can do *all* things, including praising Him. When we tap into God's strength, we can overcome our fears and praise Him confidently and boldly.

As I have continued to practice the power of praise, I have come to realize that it is not just a tool for overcoming fear at the moment but it can transform our hearts and minds. In Philippians 4:6–7, Paul writes, "Do not be anxious about anything, but in everything by prayer and supplication with thanksgiving let your requests be made known to God. And the peace of God, which surpasses all understanding, will guard your hearts and your minds in Christ Jesus" (ESV). Here, we see that when we come before God with thanksgiving and praise, He gives us His peace that surpasses all understanding.

But how does this work? How can praising God help us overcome fear and bring us inner peace?

Firstly, when we praise God, our focus shifts from ourselves and our fears to

Him. Instead of dwelling on our problems and anxieties, we are reminded of who God is and His faithfulness. This perspective shift helps us see our situations from a different angle—one grounded in trust and hope rather than fear.

Secondly, when we praise God amid fear or anxiety, we actively trust Him. This act of faith strengthens our relationship with God and deepens our understanding of His character. As a result, we are reassured that He is with us and will never leave or forsake us (Hebrews 13:5).

Praise also powerfully affects our minds. When we focus on God's goodness instead of our fears, our thoughts align with His truth. In Romans 12:2, Paul instructs us to "be transformed by the renewal of your mind" (ESV). By praising God, we can fill our minds with positive thoughts rooted in His Word rather than negative thoughts influenced by fear.

In addition to transforming our thoughts and perspectives, praise also invites God's presence into our lives. In Psalm 22:3, we are told that God is holy and inhabits the praises of His people. God inhabits *your* praise—think about how powerful that is when facing fear. God is victorious and present in every circumstance we can imagine.

Moreover, in Isaiah 41:10, God promises, "Fear not, for I am with you; be not dismayed, for I am your God; I will strengthen you, I will help you, I will uphold you with My righteous right hand" (ESV). This verse is a powerful reminder that God is always with us and will strengthen us in our times of fear. He promises to help us and uphold us with His righteous right hand. Remembering these promises, we can confidently praise God, knowing He is always with us and will help us overcome our fears.

Rom 12:1 "Therefore, I urge you brothers, in view of God's mercy, to offer your bodies as living sacrifices, holy and pleasing - this is your spiritual act of worship."

Emotions come from our flesh, not our spirit. So, while we may feel afraid, we can take comfort in knowing that God is right there with us and we have no cause for fear.

I have personally experienced the power of spiritual praise in my life. There have been times when fear has consumed me, and I have felt overwhelmed and paralyzed. But as I turned to God and began to praise Him, a supernatural peace and strength washed over me. In those moments, I was reminded of God's faithfulness and promise never to leave or forsake me. My fear dissipated with each word of praise, and I could trust in God's power to overcome complex challenges.

There are countless stories of people who have overcome fear through spiritual praise. One such story is that of Corrie ten Boom, a Christian who survived the Holocaust. In her books, she shares how she and her sister Betsie found joy and peace amid the horrors of the concentration camp through their practice of praise. Betsie became very weak and sick, and together, the sisters prayed that she would be healed. But she died in the concentration camp.

Years later, God placed Corrie face to face with one of the guards from that concentration camp. The man was seeking Corrie's forgiveness. Corrie writes, "I discovered that it is not on our forgiveness any more than on our goodness that the world's healing hinges, but on His [God's]. When He tells us to love our enemies, He gives, along with the command, the love itself."* This powerful testimony shows us we can find strength to forgive and healing through spiritual praise, even in the darkest circumstances.

The practices I propose in this guide can sometimes stir up fear. Perhaps you feel a knot in your stomach at the thought of being surrounded by strangers, their unfamiliar faces and voices overwhelming your senses. Maybe anxiety creeps in as you worry that your praise might fall short of your expectations or that your words may not blend harmoniously, failing to convey your intended message. The fear of the unknown is tangible, casting shadows as you enter uncharted territory. Yet, within you lies the strength to conquer this fear, to face it head-on and emerge victorious. If you don't trust me, trust in the promises of Jesus!

The practice of spiritual praise is a powerful weapon that we can use to overcome fear in our lives. It is not just a form of religious ritual but a spiritual discipline that strengthens our faith and trust in God. When we praise God, we declare His goodness and greatness, and our fears fade. We are reminded that God is in control and has the power to overcome any fear or obstacle in our lives. So, let us make a conscious effort to unleash a practice of spiritual praise in our lives and experience the supernatural victories that come from praising our great and mighty God.

* Corrie ten Boom, *The Hiding Place* (Peabody, MA: Hendrickson Publishers, 1971), 262.

Overcoming Fear
5 Biblical Truths

JESUS IS GREATER
THAN YOUR STORM
"even the wind and the waves obey Him."
Mark 4:39-41

GOD IS WITH YOU
"Do not fear, for I am with you"
Isaiah 41:10

PERFECT LOVE
DRIVES OUT FEAR
"There is no fear in love."
1 John 4:18

PEACE IS YOUR PROMISE
"My peace I give to you....do not let your
heart be troubled."
John 14:27

GOD HAS NOT GIVEN YOU A
SPIRIT OF FEAR....
"but of power, love and a sound mind."
2 Tim 1:7

TIME FOR CRAZY PRAISE

PERSONALIZED ENCOURAGEMENT CARDS

Get some notecards or cut out some cardboard. Write out the "overcoming fear" scriptures above, one on each card, only add your name to the scripture to remind yourself God's word is just for you! Look up some additional scriptures to write out as well.

You may want to gather together some friends and have a craft day to make these, you can even have each person make one or two cards for the others in the group. Decorate them with stickers, drawings or scrapbooking border tape to make them special.

Here is one I use myself quite a bit:

Camille, for God did not give us a spirit of feat but of power and love and self-control. - 2 Timothy 1:7

Another one I looked up on my own:

Wait for the Lord, Camille; be strong, and let your heart take courage; wait for the Lord. Psalm 27:14

Visit our website at www.crazypraiseclub.com under the Resources section to order these customized cards in a number of design options.

CREATING YOUR OWN
CRAZY PRAISE CLUB

A Personal Journey of Transformative Creative Experiences

Creating a Crazy Praise Club is an exciting venture that can unite people in unique and impactful ways to explore their faith and creativity. While you can certainly go on this journey alone, I can tell you from experience that Crazy Praise Club is best when shared with your tribe, and it can be a reason to form a tribe if you don't have one. Our CPC instructors and facilitators are here to support you along the way.

If you find yourself without an in-person group, consider joining our vibrant online CPC, where you can cultivate a sense of community in the digital realm. There are numerous opportunities to connect and engage meaningfully. If you have journeyed with me through the pages of this book, it is likely that you feel a stirring within—a desire to invigorate your faith journey with new energy. I would like to help you start on that transformative path.

The original CPC began as a small group of just four individuals, yet we were wholeheartedly devoted to nurturing our faith and supporting one another. We gathered for activities once or twice a month, amounting to around fifteen meetings yearly. Despite the limited number of gatherings, that year transformed me—and all of us—in profound and lasting ways. We witnessed the powerful and awe-inspiring work of God, and those tales remain to be told in the next book!

Here is a detailed guide on how to establish your own Crazy Praise Club and begin immersing yourself in transformative and creative experiences of praise. Below are some steps to take to begin your group, followed by sample activities to inspire you. But remember, your group can take any form that works for you, as long as it remains centered on Christ and the ultimate aim is to celebrate and uplift Him through praise!

Mission and Purpose

Objective: Crazy Praise Club's primary goal is to help people deepen their praise of and intimacy with Christ through interactive experiences. These experiences can take many forms: workshops on faith-based art, guided writing, music, dance, nature-based activities, fitness and cooking, conferences—the sky is the limit.

Focus: We emphasize personal growth, creativity, and community building. We encourage members to explore their faith innovatively and foster a supportive environment where praise can flourish. Our goal is to take every thought captive for Christ, in times of fun and laughter or times of self-reflection and sorrow.

Steps to Form a Crazy Praise Club

1. Define Your Vision

Identify Need: Understand what your community needs. Where do your potential participants want to grow in their walk with Jesus? Perhaps they feel stuck or stagnant. Possibly, they are working through grief or loss. Things may be going well, and the participants want to continue on their course. Often, they are simply looking to build community. Understanding the needs of the group will help you strategize activities.

Set Goals: Clearly outline your objectives for the club. Do you aim to strengthen individual faith journeys, inspire artistic expression, or cultivate a nurturing environment where members support one another?

Create a Safe Place: Reiterate to the group that anything you share or experience will be confidential. When someone shares a problematic part of their journey, it is essential to assure them that it will be kept in confidence.

Be Inclusive: There are so many people—many more than you realize—who are desperate for community. Even when it can be challenging, err on the side of inclusivity. You never want your group to feel cliquey or exclusive. The goal is to welcome all in with the love of Christ. I purposely try to invite people who may be on the outskirts or periphery of a small group or church, just hoping they can feel the love of the group.

NOTE: Occasionally, include activities geared toward those who are spiritually unresolved but looking for community. Service projects and art classes are great for this. When an activity might be significant for them, you can encourage group members to bring a friend. Crazy Praise Club is also about outreach!

2. Gather Your Leadership

Build a Core Team: Someone has to drive the bus, so assemble a small group of dedicated individuals to help with planning and organization. Leadership can rotate or have a couple of people designated as the leaders.

Recruit Activity Leaders: Find people with diverse talents and passions willing to lead workshops or activities. You will be surprised at the talent God will bring your way! When you have a small group, some of the shyer, more introverted people may be more comfortable stepping out and leading an activity. This can be life-changing for them, building their confidence and providing a safe place to explore their gifts. I can't tell you how many times I have seen introverted ladies open up and start sharing over an art project!

Divide up the roles so you have one person as the main communications person, one person planning and scheduling snacks, another facilitating, etc. so everyone has ownership of some piece of the experience.

Leadership Skills: It is always helpful to have some questions prepared to throw to the group to stimulate discussion. Make your questions open-ended, begin with terms like "what" or "how," and avoid yes-or-no answers. So, instead of "Did you agree with the point on _____?" you can ask, "In what ways did you agree or disagree with the point on _____?" These kinds of questions facilitate more participatory discussion. If you are facilitating, remember your role is to *guide* the group, not dominate the discussion.

Thank God for YouTube! If you want to teach a painting class, for example, and no one wants to lead, you can look at some options on YouTube and do it together. I recommend prescreening the instructor and choosing one with the skill level you desire, making up a materials list to distribute to participants (or alternatively, all chip in and one person get supplies), and situating the

TV in an area where all can see as they paint. I have done this before in a small group, and we had such a great time.

3. Plan Activities

Workshops and Events: Organize activities like art sessions, writing workshops, music nights, testimonial potluck gatherings, or nature walks. You can start by attending a church event, seminar, or painting studio and then build from there.

Another option is to find a speaker or topic of interest, gather to watch an online presentation, and share feedback. Lifeway and YouTube offer many great online speakers and courses. If you have a Bible study your group particularly liked, you may choose to find something more by that teacher.

Guest Speakers: Invite inspiring speakers to share their experiences and insights. Think about people you know with inspiring testimonies, or those who have ministries in a particular area. If the Lord puts them in your heart, they have a purpose in sharing their story with your group!

4. Secure a Venue

In the early days of CPC, we mostly met outside at a local park, our local coffee shop, or in someone's home. Many of our events focused on nature and prayer walks, so this worked perfectly. A picnic and music at the park are always fun activities everyone enjoys. The location should suit the activity, so you don't want to do the painting in a coffee shop, for example.

You don't need a formal space, especially if you're starting small. People with the gift of hospitality are usually willing to step up and host. I have had success contacting local churches and asking them to provide space.

You may decide to meet during the school year and take a summer break. One of my groups culminated in a fantastic and meaningful May retreat— fourteen people attended! After a few months off for summer, we reconvened in September and had a great turnout and new members.

Consider a mix of events where children of a certain age can participate, like a cookout or park visit, so young mothers can also have community. For small-group environments where I offer childcare, I most often draft the teenage kids of participants to watch the smaller ones. I ask parents to chip in five to ten dollars for the teen, and I have not had trouble getting childcare assistance. A trusted neighbor or friend also works. If you're meeting in the church and want to offer childcare, ask your contact at the church what their guidelines are, because they will vary from place to place.

5. Communication Framework

How will you communicate event details and prayer requests within your group? Over the years, I have been a part of many groups and seen all of these work: a Facebook group page, Facebook messenger, a Slack channel, GroupMe, email, text messages, and more. Determine what works best for the group and set it up. I have a simple information form I always give to first-time visitors, collecting their email, phone, Facebook name, and area of town where they live. I always ask what kinds of activities they enjoy. If they are new to the group, I make sure to include some of their favorite activities in my planning so they feel welcomed.

Each member of your group can take ownership of meetings by splitting up tasks. So, one person can cover communication, one coordinates food, one provides a home, and one facilitates. Rotate jobs as you see fit. Maybe you'll be blessed as I was with one person who wants to provide the food for the entire session every week!

Also, don't feel you have to provide snacks at every meeting. Depending on the time, sometimes just water is fine.

7. Build Community

Encourage members to provide feedback and suggestions for future activities. At your first gathering, ask the members to write down their hopes for two things: 1) how they will grow individually through the group, and 2) how they will grow collectively and build community through the group. Ask everyone to share and discuss these to ensure everyone's needs are met.

By following these steps and focusing on transformative experiences intended to draw all participants nearer to God through creative forms of praise, you can establish a vibrant Crazy Praise Club that inspires people to grow in their faith and creativity.

Here We Go! Transformative Creative Experiences

Here are some suggestions for activities to explore in your own Crazy Praise Club. I have personally experienced each of these activities and witnessed firsthand the positive influence they can have on people. Consider these as initial stepping stones. Every Crazy Praise Club has its unique character and spirit, so modify these ideas to suit your particular club's dynamics and preferences. While your group will share lots of moments of laughter, always be sure to have tissues on hand, as some of your meeting activities may bring up strong emotions among the participants.

These activities are accessible to everyone, allowing additional layers to be added as desired to enhance them. Generally, simplicity is most effective. A simple approach tends to make participants feel more at ease, and the workshops become enjoyable experiences rather than overwhelming tasks. For example, if you organize an art workshop, do not require participants to bring their own supplies. Instead, build an art kit for the group that you can use repeatedly. This way, the effort feels light and engaging, inviting everyone to participate without hesitation.

I recommend always having the next activity scheduled or at least in mind whenever you meet so you can plant the seeds and get on people's calendars. For my group, my co-leader and I meet over the Christmas holidays and work out the calendar for the entire next year. We post it on our Facebook group page and pin it to the top so people can reference it and get the dates on their calendars each month. No matter what dates you choose, they will present a scheduling conflict for someone. You must commit to the date that works for the most people and go with it. If you try to wait for a date that works for everyone, you may never have an event!

Be sure to start and end your sessions with prayer so the Holy Spirit is invited to be present throughout the experience. This helps your group to keep the focus on your goal, which is to deepen your praise and grow in intimacy with God.

We invite you to share photos and descriptions of your experiences on the Crazy Praise Club website so we can celebrate with you! We can't wait to see what you come up with!

Let's Ignite Your Praise!

1. Get-to-Know-You Dinner. This fun meal works for a potluck or an in-person cooking event and is a great vehicle for informally building Christian community as you get to know one another. Ask each person to present a dish that reflects who they are, perhaps a favorite family recipe, something they particularly enjoy, or a regional favorite from where they grew up. As each person narrates the story behind their dish, it sparks engaging conversations that enrich the dining experience. This event can also be transformed into a festive holiday celebration by asking each guest to bring a dish that holds a special place on their traditional holiday table, adding layers of nostalgia and warmth to the occasion. For a fun twist, ask participants to relate their dish to a Scripture.

The beauty of fellowship, building community around Christ, and appreciating one another's faith walk is cause for thanksgiving and praise. When God leads us together, good things happen!

2. Worship through Art. Explore spiritual themes through visual art such as painting, drawing, collage, or pottery. Play worship music in the background as participants create. You can get supplies inexpensively at Hobby Lobby or WalMart or order them on Amazon. If you don't have an artist in your group, there are many YouTube instructional videos for painting. My small group did a YouTube video painting session, which was hilarious—there were lots of pauses in the instruction and tons of laughter. Your group leader will want to watch the entire video beforehand to ensure it won't be too challenging and that it fits within a godly framework. These can be very moving sessions, especially for people working through grief or loss.

3. Journal Making and Spiritual Writing. It is very satisfying to personalize your own journal using decoupage techniques. Encourage the group to bring images from books, magazines, and scrapbooking. There are many different ways to make journals. Our website features videos on a couple of our favorite methods. I like to finish these workshops with a guided exercise in which participants write their own psalm in their journal. If participants are comfortable doing so, ask them to share their journals and their psalm. I usually end up crying through these sessions—they can be so moving.

4. Worship through Music and Movement. Host music nights that center around music. One of my favorite themes is a nostalgic throwback night featuring those worship songs that once echoed through our hearts but have since faded from regular rotation. These selections were incredibly inspirational at one time of our lives, and they spark memories of past spiritual journeys. Create a playlist filled with these songs and provide printed lyrics so everyone can sing along and immerse themselves fully in the experience. This forms a great basis for group discussion. It is a big plus if the host has a good sound system. If you are lucky enough to have a musician in your circle, the guitar's strum or piano's gentle notes can elevate the praise with live music.

Participants can take their musical worship even further by bringing in movement, such as dance or sign language. I recently saw a workshop where participants painted silk scarves and then danced to the Lord using their creations—now *that's* crazy praise!

5. *Worship Stations.* Set up stations where individuals can engage in various activities (art, prayer, music, Communion). It can be fun to do the stations in pairs or teams. CPC does a sensory workshop where we explore the sights, sounds, tastes, smells (essential oils), and touches of biblical times using stations. You can assign each group member a different station. At the end, let each person share how the Lord touched them at each station and their big takeaway.

6. *Nature Prayer Walks.* Organize outdoor activities connecting faith and nature. As nature is a primary spiritual pathway for many, the outdoors is a great environment in which to connect with God in prayer and observe His creativity. Create a guided prayer walk with specific prompts at various points to facilitate reflection. Select a new park or location where the group has never been. This will heighten your senses because you'll see everything for the first time. I recommend taking small notebooks and pens to record prayers, observations, and any whispers from the Holy Spirit. I like to do these on Saturday mornings and then have lunch together to share what the Lord showed us.

7. *Scavenger Hunt.* Create a scavenger hunt to find God in unexpected places by hiding Scripture verses around a location, or lead participants to find objects, such as a cross on a store item or a mother and child, prompting reflection and discussion. Be creative in finding God where you least expect Him. Offer fun little prizes for the fastest, the one who makes the funniest comments, etc. Have each person select one of the Scriptures and ask them to relate it to their lives.

8. *Testimony Night and Community Building.* It is always amazing how I can socialize with the same group of people for a long time without knowing their

testimonies. When you set aside time and give each person ten to fifteen minutes to share, you will be amazed at how this deepens relationships. Focus the night's conversation on how God was right there with them through every step of their journey and how He used their experiences to draw them closer to Himself.

9. Communion Service. Create a special space with candles, a Bible, and instrumental worship music for a communal Communion ceremony. Before participating, establish a solemn atmosphere by encouraging members to search their hearts for any unconfessed sin, unforgiveness, or wrong attitudes they want God to work on within them. Serve Communion to one another. The reverence and awe that one can experience during Communion can be very emotional for the participants. Occasionally, I suggest people depart silently after Communion to contemplate what God has revealed.

10. Service Projects. There is no better way to minimize your challenges than to serve others. Organize community-service projects that blend creativity with the spirit of giving back. Select a project that is meaningful to your group. Imagine leading art projects at a senior center, for example, bringing color and joy to the residents' days. My small group enjoys preparing Christmas and Easter treats for local foster kids and college students who can't travel home. We've given out food, prepared meal kits for overseas, delivered gifts, provided music at senior centers, and cleaned up hiking trails to serve hikers. Choose a project that resonates with group members or relates to a church project. In these acts of kindness, we embody the hands and feet of Christ, spreading His love and compassion through our actions!

11. Conquering Fears. Talk through, work through, and pray through things that scare members of your group. I was deathly afraid of heights, so imagine my surprise (not in a good way!) when the other CPC members whisked me away to ride an enormous Ferris wheel towering over the bustling cityscape of downtown Atlanta! It was their unique way of helping me face my fear of heights. They kept our destination a secret until the very last moment. As we approached the colossal structure, its brightly colored cabins slowly rotated against the city skyline. My heart raced with excitement and dread. With their unwavering support and encouragement, I managed to step into one of the swaying cabins and complete the ride without fainting—a personal triumph that felt like soaring through the clouds!

12. Leave obstacles behind. Host a gathering where we everyone shares some current challenges or fears they are facing in their faith walk. Inscribe all these personal obstacles onto slips of paper and then ceremonially burn them in a small bonfire. The flames dance upwards, symbolically marking a profound shift in your spirits from being ensnared by fear to embracing faith and turning your hearts toward God as the One who will enable you to have an overcomers spirit. For extra drama, when you exit the firepit area, instruct everyone to not look back, but to only look ahead and leave behind the ashes of everything holding you back.

Honestly, there are so many possibilities for how you can praise Jesus in new ways. This list is just the beginning. The goal is to get you thinking about imaginative ways you can grow in your faith that are unique to your group and new ways to share praise experiences with others.

Conclusion: Ignite the Power of Transformative Praise

As you prepare to step into your own Crazy Praise Club experience, the echoes of the laughter, tears, and triumphs that blessed me on my own journey remind me of the profound impact that transformative praise can have on our lives. The original club, born from a desire to connect faith and creativity, has become a testament to the power of community and the unbridled joy of praising God in innovative ways.

As I close, I'm inspired by the incredible journey the original members of CPC embarked on in those early days, never dreaming what a catalyst it would become for healing, discovery, and praise. Our lives have changed so much, yet we are forever bound together by the growth we found as a group of loving friends. Our collective prayer is that, in some small way, everything we experienced then and are still pursuing now will inspire your journey of faith. After all, *you* (and Jesus!) are the hero of your own story of praise.

Throughout our CPC history, we have witnessed people from diverse backgrounds come together, each with unique stories and struggles. Yet, as we ventured on this creative journey, we discovered that praise as a form of worship is a catalyst for transformation. Praise is the thread that weaves our experiences into a tapestry of hope, resilience, and joy. I honor every person who has joined us on our journey thus far, and I honor you as you go forth on your Crazy Praise Club journey.

Praise in all its forms—whether through art, writing, learning, health, storytelling, or any other creative expression—has proven to be a potent force for change. It lifts spirits, heals wounds, and brings people closer to their faith and each other. The Crazy Praise Club has shown us that when we praise, even in the darkest moments, we open ourselves to a deeper connection with God and those around us.

Your Community of Support

One of the most remarkable aspects of this journey is the sense of community that can develop. People who once felt isolated or alone can find a supportive network where they can share their stories, fears, and triumphs. This community becomes a sanctuary where they can be themselves without fear of judgment and grow together in faith and creativity.

In joining with the Crazy Praise Club team, with our online presence and wealth of resources at your disposal, you will never again feel alone. You will have access to a community that loves you enough to inspire you to grow continually. More importantly, as will be the case in eternity, you will be part of the larger community of Christ followers who are forever united by their supreme desire to praise without ceasing.

A Legacy of Joy

As I close this chapter, I am reminded that the true legacy of the Crazy Praise Club is not just the experiences that we share but the joy that we discover along the journey. It is the knowledge that no matter what challenges lie ahead, we can transform them and be transformed ourselves through praise. We march forward with the authority and identity of Jesus. Our joy is contagious, spreading from heart to heart, and it will continue to inspire and uplift all who are a part of this journey.

Ultimately, what defines us are not grand gestures or dramatic moments but the small acts of praise and gratitude we practice daily. Though simple, these acts have the power to transform our lives and the lives of those around us. As we move forward, let us carry the spirit of the Crazy Praise Club with us, spreading joy, hope, and transformative praise wherever we go.

Your journey of transformative praise is just beginning. May it be a source of strength, inspiration, and joy for you. Until we meet again, stay joyful and hopeful, and always remember to *keep transforming your heart with crazy praise!*

TIME FOR CRAZY PRAISE

OUR CRAZY PRAISE CLUB

NAME:

VISION FOR OUR GROUP:

GROUP GOALS:

CORE LEADERS AND AREAS OF RESPONSIBILITY:

ACTIVITIES TO PLAN & WHO IS RESPONSIBLE

TIMETABLE AND METHOD FOR GATHERING

HOW WILL WE COMMUNICATE?

HOW WILL BE BUILD COMMUNITY?

CREATIVE DIRECTION WE WILL TAKE -

ART ICONS OR SYMBOLS WE WANT TO USE -

AFTERWORD

As you close the final pages of *Joyful Hearts – The Transformative Power of Praise*, my prayer is that something stirred in your spirit – a spark of joy, a shift in perspective, a renewed passion for praising God in every season of life.

This book was born out of a deep desire to encourage believers – especially people like you – to rediscover the beauty and power of praise. Not the kind of praise reserved for Sunday mornings alone, but the kind that weaves itself into the fabric of everyday life. The kind of praise that lifts heavy hearts, realigns weary souls, and declares God's goodness in the midst of chaos.

I know this power firsthand.

There was a season in my life when darkness felt closer than light. I was shackled by the shame of my choices, burdened, confused and battling a deep weariness in my soul. When I was in that place, the Holy Spirit gently reminded me to praise. Not because I felt like it, but because God was still worthy. I began to lift my voice in the quiet darkness, to sing in the storm, and to speak truth over my emotions. And little by little, joy returned. Peace returned. Hope returned. That's when it hit me: praise is not a response to our feelings, it's a weapon for our freedom.

Praise has the incredible power to give hope in the face of hopelessness. After all, we are only here for a little while, and my hope is anchored in the life to come, the one shared with my Savior, Jesus. When we praise, we are able to abandon, if only briefly, those things that can tether us to worry and shame. And when we are struggling, that hope is often the single thing we can hang on to.

I'm often asked about the original Crazy Praise Club members. Some of those people are still among my closest friends. Some have moved on in their journey and life circumstances have drawn them in different directions. But I can say that every single one of them, then and now, has embraced their faith in new and exciting ways. That year we spent together was a moment in time that we will forever remember, and we can all look back and celebrate how far we've come.

Writing *Joyful Hearts* was not just a literary journey, but a profoundly spiritual one. As I wrote, I wept, worshipped, waited and listened. And now, I pass it on to you with the hope that it becomes so much more than just a book on your shelf. May it become an essential companion in your faith walk, a reminder that you are not alone, and a testimony that joy and hope truly can rise from ashes when we praise through the pain.

If this message has resonated with you, I want to personally invite you to stay connected. Your story matters. Join our growing community of Spirit-filled women who are choosing joy, walking in faith, and praising God through every season of life. So tell a friend. Start a small group. Our original Crazy Praise Club was only four people, it doesn't take much to begin your journey. Use your voice to spread the hope and healing that praise brings. Be the light of Jesus to a world that needs joyful hearts now more than ever.

ACKNOWLEDGMENTS

First and foremost, I give all glory to God, who has been my strength and guide throughout this journey. Without His wisdom and grace, this book would not have been possible. I want to thank my chosen family for their unwavering support, encouragement, and prayers. Your belief in me always has been a source of inspiration. And to my readers, thank you for taking the Crazy Praise Club journey alongside me. My prayer is that this book will be a blessing to you as it has been to me.

This book benefits from the creative contributions of several talented people. I want to acknowledge the work of editorial consultant Michelle Shelfer in helping to guide the writing, grammar and editorial content of this book. Thanks go to graphic designer Lydia Hall, who worked hard on the cover and interior design of the book. And what an honor it's been to work alongside the talented writer and artist Ashley Rogers, who contributed illustrations and is involved in future Joyful Hearts projects.

Certain writers, pastors, and educators have significantly inspired and influenced me, and I feel compelled to acknowledge their influence on this work. I'll start with Dr. Caroline Leaf, a neuroscientist whose book *Switch On Your Brain* was a foundational influence for this work. Pastor Louie Giglio's writing and teachings have deeply inspired me and impacted my life. Pastor Dan Reiland, a fantastic writer and teacher, kindly encouraged me when I shared my vision for this ministry. And author Gary Thomas and his book *Sacred Pathways* also inspired my journey. And, at a more personal level, my own Pastor Rico Ruiz and his wife Vikki have believed in this project and been sensitive to Holy Spirit prompts to help it come to life.

I extend my heartfelt gratitude to my dear friend and writing mentor, talented author Carole Townsend, whose influence has been a guiding star in my creative journey. Her example ignited a spark within me to aim for the stars. She refused to let me falter when I was ready to abandon this project. With unwavering determination, she called me tenaciously, urging me to put pen to paper, to tell my story, and to release this creation into the world. This book would not have come to fruition without her relentless encouragement. Thank you, sweet friend, for being the gentle, yet persistent, force that propelled me forward.

My cherished friend Donna Whitten Dibble believed so sincerely in this project that, over a decade ago, she took the thoughtful step of purchasing the URL for me one day over coffee when I was facing a profound disappointment. Her unwavering support has been a guiding light on my journey ever since. When she invited me to join her writer's group over a year ago, she unknowingly ignited a passionate flame within me, and this book is the result. I'm forever grateful.

I am profoundly grateful to my sister in Christ, Amy South. She has repeatedly reached out with uplifting words during the most trying seasons of my life. Amy is a beacon of joy, a tireless spreader of happiness and positivity. As my small-group leader, she guides with wisdom and grace; as my business partner, she brings insight and dedication; and as my lifelong friend, she offers unwavering support. Her presence in my life is an immense blessing. She stands by me through every hurdle, instilling a belief in myself that transforms my journey.

I am grateful to my dear friend Chris Dilworth, whose unwavering support has strengthened me through all my wild and imaginative endeavors. Her ability to lift my spirits with laughter during my lowest moments is unmatched, and her readiness to create joyful memories whenever needed is genuinely invaluable. Her incredible sons, Tanner and Keaton, have consistently encouraged and assisted me, serving as dependable sources of motivation and aid throughout my journey. What a blessing this family has been to me.

My friend, Kyle Horton, is a true beacon of light. She listens with an open heart, without even a hint of judgment, always reflecting genuine empathy and understanding. When she offers advice, it is both sound and direct, a perfect blend of spiritual insight that touches the soul and practical assessment that grounds me in reality. Her words are like a guiding compass, always pointing me in the right direction. She has lent her business acumen to this journey but mostly lent her incredible kindness and practical support to my crazy dreams.

Acknowledgments

My Watch and Write Christian Writer's Group has rallied behind this project, offered guidance and contacts to bring it to life, and has been a valuable accountability group throughout this journey. Each of them is wildly talented and incredibly busy in their own right, yet they take time to encourage and inform my journey.

Gramma, I wish you were here to experience this with me. I miss you every day, and this book is the result of all the love you poured into me throughout my life. When I was little, you always told me I could do anything I put my mind to. When I told you I wanted to write a book, you said I could do it. I believed you. One day, I promise to bring a copy to you in heaven so you can see what your belief in me helped create. I hope it makes you proud.

ABOUT THE AUTHOR

Camille Burch is a devoted Christian writer, speaker, teacher and leader who loves creating actionable content and videos to help others grow in their faith. Through books, blogs, ministry activities, or events, Camille and the talented Crazy Praise Club team seek to make God's Word relevant and accessible in everyday life. With a heart for discipleship, Camille is committed to igniting hearts for praise through biblical truths, personal growth, and a strong community.

With a professional background in marketing, writing, and event management, Camille is taking that expertise, coupled with the expertise of a hand-picked advisory board, to launch Crazy Praise Club. The ministry is dedicated to developing creative interactive resources from a variety of contributors to ignite faith through the praise of Jesus!

Crazy Praise Club was born in a small group in 2013. Since then, their platform of creative events has reached small groups, conferences, and online platforms, encouraging women to walk boldly in their faith and identity in Christ. At the Holy Spirit's prompting, the ministry and content are now moving to a broader audience. This book is an important step in that vision.

Camille resides in a suburb of Atlanta, Georgia where she is actively involved in church, the Tres Dias community, small groups and her Christian writing group. She enjoys hosting painting and writing events in her home, entertaining friends with dinner parties, and exploring new creative ways to praise. Her greatest passion is facilitating spiritual growth in others in any way she can, including through the online platform.

Visit www.crazypraiseclub.com or our Facebook/Meta group page, Crazy Praise Club, for more information and the latest resources.

www.ingramcontent.com/pod-product-compliance
Lightning Source LLC
Chambersburg PA
CBHW021647120626
46545CB00002B/744